The Tyndale New Testament Commentaries

General Editor: PROFESSOR

THE ACTS OF THE APOSTLES

THE ACTS
OF THE APOSTLES

AN HISTORICAL COMMENTARY

by

E. M. BLAIKLOCK, Litt.D.

Professor of Classics, Auckland University
New Zealand

Wm. B. Eerdmans Publishing Company
Grand Rapids, Michigan

First Edition — March 1959
Fifth printing — March 1974
Sixth printing — March 1975

Library of Congress Catalog Card Number: 59-8752

PHOTOLITHOPRINTED BY GRAND RAPIDS BOOK MANUFACTURERS, INC.
GRAND RAPIDS, MICHIGAN

GENERAL PREFACE

ALL who are interested in the teaching and study of the New Testament today cannot fail to be concerned with the lack of commentaries which avoid the extremes of being unduly technical or unhelpfully brief. It is the hope of the editor and publishers that this present series will do something towards the supply of this deficiency. Their aim is to place in the hands of students and serious readers of the New Testament, at a moderate cost, commentaries by a number of scholars who, while they are free to make their own individual contributions, are united in a common desire to promote a truly biblical theology.

The commentaries are primarily exegetical and only secondarily homiletic, though it is hoped that both student and preacher will find them informative and suggestive. Critical questions are fully considered in introductory sections, and also, at the author's discretion, in additional notes.

The commentaries are based on the Authorized (King James) Version, partly because this is the version which most Bible readers possess, and partly because it is easier for commentators, working on this foundation, to show why, on textual and linguistic grounds, the later versions are so often to be preferred. No one translation is regarded as infallible, and no single Greek manuscript or group of manuscripts is regarded as always right! Greek words are transliterated to help those unfamiliar with the language, and to save those who do know Greek the trouble of discovering what word is being discussed.

There are many signs today of a renewed interest in what the Bible has to say and of a more general desire to understand its meaning as fully and clearly as possible. It is the hope of all those concerned with this series that God will graciously use what they have written to further this end.

R. V. G. TASKER.

CHIEF ABBREVIATIONS

AV	English Authorized Version (King James).
RV	English Revised Version, 1881.
RSV	American Revised Standard Version, 1946.
Blunt	*Acts* by A. W. F. Blunt (Clarendon Bible), 1923.
Bruce	*The Acts of the Apostles* by F. F. Bruce (Commentary on the Greek Text), 1951.
Conybeare and Howson	*The Life and Epistles of Saint Paul* by W. J. Conybeare and J. S. Howson, 1852.
Farrar	*The Life and Work of Saint Paul* by F. W. Farrar, 1879.
Foakes-Jackson	*The Acts of the Apostles* by F. J. Foakes-Jackson (Moffatt New Testament Commentaries), 1931.
Knowling	*Acts* by R. J. Knowling (Expositor's Greek Testament), 1900.
Lumby	*Acts* by J. R. Lumby (Cambridge Greek Testament), 1894.
Rackham	*The Acts of the Apostles* by R. B. Rackham (Westminster Commentaries), 1902.
Ramsay	*The Church in the Roman Empire* by W. M. Ramsay, 1895. *The Cities of Saint Paul* by W. M. Ramsay, 1907. *Luke the Physician* by W. M. Ramsay, 1908. *Pauline Studies* by W. M. Ramsay, 1906. *St. Paul the Traveller and Roman Citizen* by W. M. Ramsay, 1896. *The Teaching of Paul in Terms of the Present Day* by W. M. Ramsay, 1914.

CONTENTS

ACKNOWLEDGEMENT

Scripture quotations from the Revised Standard Version of the Bible (copyrighted 1946 and 1952 by the Division of Christian Education, National Council of Churches, U.S.A.) are used by permission.

AUTHOR'S PREFACE

IT is Easter Saturday, and since mid-December Luke the historian has been my constant companion. His purposeful Greek has grown familiar to my ear. I have learned a little to read between his lines. I have caught the warmth of his life's enthusiasm, that admiration for a great and noble-minded friend which took him twice across the sea.

Luke's book has shared my summer travels. I think he might have been glad to see it in my hand on the last southern ledge of the world's habitable shores, in a region Caesar never knew. It would have moved him to hear a text of Paul expounded on Christmas Day at Pounawea, where the Catlins and Owaka Rivers join forces to meet the breakers of the empty sea which extends from New Zealand's remotest south to the Antarctic ice.

Tonight the last word of commentary was written in the autumn twilight. Were I a Roman poet I should ask in hendecasyllables: 'To whom shall I give my little book?' To whom? To students, with the wish that it may make more vital and more clear one of the most significant works of ancient literature; to the busy and preoccupied of this distracted age, with the hope that one, whose dearest privilege it has been to live professionally amid the thoughts and thinkers of the Greek and Roman world, may have been able to touch with newer life a record which for many concerns a strange, unfamiliar age, and lies embalmed in unfamiliar speech; to all who seek afresh the springs of faith, with the prayer that this pen's delving may have uncovered the pure flow.

E. M. BLAIKLOCK.

Titirangi, Auckland.
April 5, 1958.

9

INTRODUCTION

I. THE BOOK

THE Acts of the Apostles is one of the most important and influential books of all time. It forms an essential link between the four records of the ministry of Christ, and the documents which interpret that ministry to the world at large. It begins in the strange and moving afterglow of the Gospels, and the closing events of the divine intervention into the history of mankind. It shows those who had known and watched that great event emerging from the ordeal which concluded it, filled with a triumphant faith, touched with new power, and realizing with exultation the role they had to play, the task they were called upon to undertake, and the message with which they were charged.

The story moves rapidly from episode to episode. It shows the Church in birth and being, and in experiment and action, as devoted minds sought after and apprehended truth, shaping policy and purpose in the process. It reveals the growing vitality of the Christian faith as it outgrew prejudice and limitation. It tells of men, who had known horizons little wider than those of Palestine, conceiving bold projects of world evangelism, and moving out in the strength of indomitable faith to reach the nations with their story.

As the purpose of the story takes final shape, it tells also of other men, for they were not dead who had misconceived the ministry of Christ and failed to see the truth which lay in centuries of Scripture. Pride and prejudice, and the preconceptions of nationalism not only attacked the new society, but penetrated it, and sought to confine and to constrict its purpose. But there was a wider world than that which was hemmed between the desert and the sea with Jerusalem as its proud, hard core. New personalities appear, singled out by the narrative, as history, too, was singling them out, men of two worlds, enriched by the faith of Judaism, but broadened by the Greeks, and with a vision of wider humanity.

Like some great drama which has delayed its hero's entry until the stage is ready and the atmosphere prepared, the Acts of the Apostles turns to Paul of Tarsus, and the book becomes, as its further chapters unfold, the Acts of Paul. The story of that great man, human, exciting, valiant, and immeasurably significant, moves to its first climax in the capital of Empire, as the book concludes.

It seems certain that a sequel was intended, but whether or not some personal catastrophe, preoccupation, or change of purpose prevented its writing, and left the Acts of the Apostles tantalizingly cut short on the eve of Paul's interview with the ruler of the world, the story is not inappropriately interrupted at that point. The ministry of Paul was not bounded by the limits of a life. It influenced decisively all European history, and through European history the history of the whole modern world. Paul's was the most significant human life ever lived, and when he came to Rome, the purpose for which he had toiled and striven was virtually achieved.

The Acts of the Apostles, cut short yet complete, is the story of that consummation. Christ was for the world, and by the faith and courage of one man above all others, that gift was made certain and inalienable. The writer of Acts holds that thought like a jewel of price. As his story unfolds he employs every art and device of narrative to show that God's purpose was as wide as his friend envisaged it. Even before the great figure from Tarsus steps into the story, it is suggested in a dozen ways that something had happened in Palestine of which the world was to hear, and that what had been done there had been done in no corner. The final sweep of the great story took logical flight from its first beginnings.

Vivid, rapid in its movement, sure and purposeful in brief summary or leisurely report, amazingly evocative of atmosphere, economical of words, but never drab in colour, the book holds the reader from its dedication to the end. It is only as the last chapter closes that the reader realizes whither his mind and heart have been led. It is a journey from a mysterious and haunted world, from an environment which they only knew who had known Christ, who had seen with eyes amazed the empty tomb, and who had shared the special privilege of the Spirit's first visitation, on to a world of familiar things where flesh and blood battle with wind and wave, with man-made trial and tyranny, and the perplexities of circumstance. Somehow the reader feels adequate to move on from here, for this is his world, his task, and the service of his Christ. Perhaps the purpose of a great book is fulfilled if it leaves its reader thus.

II. THE WRITER OF THE BOOK

Evidence which may be regarded as conclusive supports the view held commonly by the Church since the middle of the second century, that the Acts of the Apostles was written by Luke, the physician-friend and fellow-traveller of Paul.

External evidence is far from negligible. The oldest extant list of New Testament writings, known from the name of its discoverer as the Muratorian Fragment, and dating from the latter half of the second century, lists the third Gospel and the Acts of the Apostles as the work of Luke the physician. Irenaeus (*c*. AD 130–*c*. 200) and Clement of Alexandria (*c*. AD 150–*c*. 215) may be quoted in support. Origen (*c*. AD 185–*c*. 254) and Tertullian (*c*. AD 160–*c*. 200) bear the same testimony. A living tradition can span a century, and if, therefore, scholars about AD 170 believed that Luke wrote the Acts of the Apostles, their witness cannot be lightly dismissed.

Internal evidence coincides. First, it is clear, and generally admitted, that whoever wrote the third Gospel also wrote the Acts of the Apostles. Analysis of style and language places this matter beyond dispute. Secondly, the evidence of archaeology and epigraphy also points with increasing cogency to an author personally familiar with the world of the first century. Thirdly, that person was also a physician. His language has been exhaustively examined, and there is no doubt that there is a colouring of expression and a habit of vocabulary consistent only with a close acquaintance with Greek medical terminology. Set beside the fact that the traditional author was, in fact, a physician (Col. iv. 14), this evidence seems conclusive. Fourthly, a plain reading of the text makes it clear that the writer was a companion of Paul in certain of his travels and adventures. In four passages of varying length he writes in the first person (xvi. 10–17, xx. 5–15, xxi. 1–18, xxvii. 1–xxviii. 16). These passages, on demonstrable linguistic grounds, cannot be dissociated from the rest of the book. In other words, the writer of Acts was the writer of the whole of Acts, including the 'we-sections'. Nor, among the close associates of Paul, is an alternative available. Acts xx. 5 and 6 appear to exclude Timothy. Timothy was among those waiting for the author at Troas. Neither Titus, a shadowy figure, nor Silas were with Paul on the journey to Rome, or in Rome, and the eyewitness character of these concluding chapters of the book is beyond dispute.

All in all, it would be difficult to find a book in the whole range of ancient literature concerning which a stronger case can be made in support of a traditional authorship. That case has, in fact, been disputed only by those preoccupied on other grounds with establishing a later date than that which is consistent with a Lucan authorship—a species of scholarship happily moribund today.

Of Luke himself little is known. The author who could deliberately turn from the artificial style of his prologue to write his Gospel and its sequel in a strong and effective vernacular was a person not likely to reveal himself too intimately in his work. Tradition has it that he was a native of Antioch, but certain features of the narrative of Philippi make it very likely that he was a native of the Macedonian colony. If not, he was in all likelihood an Antiochene of Macedonian origin, who worked in Philippi for significant years. Beyond this nothing is known. He must have been a man of singular sweetness of character to earn Paul's adjective 'beloved' (Col.

iv. 14). His sympathetic treatment of Paul's adventures, and his unquestioning acceptance of the apostle's leadership, even after the rejection of earnest advice, indicate a person of self-effacing and courageous loyalty. His intellectual capacity is revealed in his work. It is conceived as a unity and the narrative drives straight to its goal. Luke was a man with an unusual capacity for research, and the scholar's ability to strip away irrelevant or dispensable detail. He had an unerring feeling for the significant, an eye for colour and character, and he could tell a story with vividness and clarity. Beyond this he is sought in vain in the pages of his books. In the 'former treatise' he preferred to make his Master prominent; in the latter, his distinguished friend.

III. THE DATE OF THE BOOK

Converging lines of evidence preclude a second-century date. The sure touch of the writer in matters of nomenclature, his eyewitness command of detail and feeling for atmosphere, his view of Rome and the imperial administration, so obviously free from the tone of censure and hostility which marks the Apocalypse, all combine to make it certain that Acts could not have been written after the organized attack on the Church instituted by Domitian (AD 81–96).

There are possible references to the text of Acts extending from the *Epistle of Barnabas* (*c.* AD 100) to Justin Martyr (*c.* AD 150) and beyond. Clement quotes the logion of Christ, mentioned in xx. 35, as early as AD 95, though of course it is always possible that he had the saying from another source. It seems clear that writers of the first half of the second century were acquainted with the book.

It has been alleged on quite insufficient grounds that Luke was familiar with the *Antiquities* of Flavius Josephus, published about AD 93. If this point could be proved it would follow that Acts must have been written in the middle nineties. This would raise two serious difficulties. First, the attitude towards the Roman administration, mentioned above; and secondly, the fact that Paul's letters do not seem to be known to Luke.

These documents were collected and generally circulated about AD 90.

A case for the early composition of Acts, say in the early sixties, rests on several grounds. First, the fresh and vivid writing of the biographical portions of the book, the so-called 'we-sections'. It does not seem reasonable to suppose that such passages were written long after the events described. Once grant the Lucan authorship of the book, and it seems likely that Luke worked upon the latter part of his narrative during the two years at Rome. This would also account for the termination of the book at that point, although this argument is admittedly weakened by the hypothesis favoured above that a third 'treatise' was intended. Secondly, if the earlier chapters of Acts depend upon researches conducted in Palestine, and the evidence of those still living who were associated with the beginnings of the Church, Caesarea provided location and occasion for such investigations, and the first part of Acts could have been written at that time. Thirdly, it is sometimes stated that the fact that the fall and devastation of Jerusalem in AD 70 left no mark upon the narrative, is an argument for composition before that date, or even before the Jewish insurrection in AD 66. No weight or little weight can be given to this argument. Luke, an accomplished historian and a disciplined writer, need not have coloured his narrative of doings in Jerusalem by references to later events irrelevant to his theme. The cogent arguments for an early date lie elsewhere.

The question of date and authorship are closely associated. If Luke wrote Acts, and that fact is beyond reasonable dispute, he wrote rather earlier than later. This was the belief of the early Church, and tradition is not without significance or importance. Critics who admit that the date cannot have been later than the outbreak of the persecution of Domitian, are sometimes in favour of a date between AD 70 and 80 because of the alleged idealization of the picture of the early Christian community in Palestine. It is contended in this commentary that such 'idealization' is imaginary. Luke's account is realistic, stresses faults and shortcomings, recounts abortive policies, and generally reveals a community coming down to earth and to reality from the witness and experience of unique events. On the whole a date in the neighbourhood of AD 62 seems reasonable.

IV. THE SOURCES OF THE BOOK

Large sections of the second half of the book are the report of an eyewitness. The account of events in Philippi in chapter xvi, and that of the two voyages in chapters xx, xxi and xxvii, xxviii read like leaves from a personal diary. The use of the first person pronoun claims this authenticity.

Events between chapters xxi and xxvii, where no personal participation is claimed, nevertheless fell within the orbit of Luke's immediate knowledge, and are recounted either with the authority of an eyewitness, or directly from the reports of those who were present in person. Paul probably had his speeches in manuscript.

Events falling between chapters xvi and xx were not remote from Luke's personal knowledge. He was at Philippi, but may from time to time have been with Paul, and could have visited Thessalonica, Athens, Corinth and Ephesus. In any case there was some coming and going of the apostolic company, and Silas, Timothy, Titus, Apollos and Aristarchus appear to have moved about a good deal; Erastus, Sopater, Tychichus and Trophimus are also mentioned. Communications were safe and well established, and emigration was common. Lydia of Thyatira was domiciled at Philippi. Apollos moved from Alexandria to Ephesus and thence to Corinth. Aquila had been born in Pontus, moved to Italy, where he met and married Priscilla, and then, under pressure of events, moved to Corinth. Timothy came from Lystra, and Barnabas from Cyprus. At Philippi Luke would have abundant opportunity of collecting first-hand information on the progress of the Church.

The story of the first missionary journey in chapters xiii and xiv, and that portion of the second journey which brought Paul into Luke's personal acquaintance at Philippi, found a ready source in Paul himself, in Timothy and Silas. Paul's speech at Lystra, a species of first draft of his Athenian oration, may have existed in manuscript.

For the events of the Jerusalem council (chapter xv) there were many authorities, but Paul is no doubt the chief source. It is most unlikely that he did not make and keep by him a detailed memorandum of events and decisions so vital to his policy.

Whether Luke was an Antiochene, as an ancient tradition maintains, or a Philippian, as some have deduced, there is no doubt that he knew the church at Antioch, and had access to many of its leading members. It was simple for him to collect accurate information concerning the doings of that influential and enterprising community (xi. 19–30, xii. 25–xiii. 3, xiv. 26–xv. 2, xv. 22–40).

At Antioch (xiii. 1) Luke must have been in touch with Barnabas, Simeon Niger and Lucius (the sources of drastically condensed information recorded in iv. 36, 37, ix. 26–30, xi. 20), with Manaen, the chief authority for brief notices of the Herod family (xii. 20–23, xxv. 13), and of course with Paul himself, who must be set down as the sole authority for events of which he so frequently spoke, those of Stephen's ministry and martyrdom, and his own conversion (recorded in chapters vii, viii and ix).

A vivid account of Philip's ministry is interpolated in chapter viii, appropriately following the story of Stephen. Philip himself, with whom Luke resided at Caesarea, must be regarded as the source of this narrative. This connection also accounts for the detailed account of the founding of the Christian communities on the Philistine coast (viii. 40, ix. 32–xi. 18). Peter, whom Luke could have met at Antioch, could be the personal source for his part in that story (chapter x). So vital was Peter's adventure of evangelism to the policy of Paul, that Paul may also have retained a detailed account of it among his 'parchments' (2 Tim. iv. 13).

Since Philip was one of 'the seven', chapter vi. 1–7 would also be based on his personal account and information. Philip, like Mnason, who next entertained Paul and Luke, was an original disciple (xxi. 8, 16), and his knowledge of the first events of Church history would be conveniently at hand to the eager historian. Mark was also available, and his personal narrative may account for the vivid story of Peter's imprisonment and deliverance, the human climax and conclusion of which probably took place in Mark's own home (xii. 3–17).

At the beginning of his Gospel Luke speaks of sundry written accounts of events surrounding the ministry of the Lord. It is more than likely that those records contained accounts of the ascension, the Pentecostal visitation and the first triumphant evangelism, events which would appear to follow naturally from the narratives of the resurrection, and indeed form confirmatory evidence. The episodic nature of chapters i–v suggests that Luke may have drawn upon such written records for the earlier incidents of his history. R. B. Rackham[1] suggests that John may have been the first historian of the Church, and supports his suggestion by an effective analysis of style and language. It must be admitted that the narrative style of the first chapters of Acts is not without similarities to that of the fourth Gospel.

The speeches of Acts are genuine reports of what was said. This is not to claim that they form a verbatim record, and are without traces of Luke's own rendering or the individual peculiarities of his style. The speeches are not, however, conceived after the fashion of Thucydides and other ancient historians, with whom the reported oration was a device for filling in the psychological background of the narrative. Such a theory called for plausibility rather than accuracy. Thucydides claims that he 'kept as closely as possible to the general tenor of what was said',[2] but his speeches are designed rather to make plain 'those subjective elements which cannot easily be displayed in an impartial narrative, but are indispensable to a proper understanding of events'.[3] Luke's

---

[1] *The Acts of the Apostles*, Introduction, p. xliii.
[2] i. 22.
[3] C. E. M. Bowra, *Ancient Greek Literature*, p. 141.

speeches, on the contrary, are reports. They bear the marks of such authenticity. They are proper to the occasion, coloured by local circumstances, bear the marks of the individual speaker, and are based, like the narrative, on personal or first-hand reports.

V. THE WORLD OF THE BOOK

a. The Roman Empire

Inescapable in the story of the Acts of the Apostles are the Romans, the rulers of the Mediterranean world. There were empires and continents beyond the reach of Rome, peoples savage and civilized who had never heard of the city by the Tiber, but the world of the first century, as history must ever view it, was the Roman world, based on the Inland Sea.

On the map of the modern globe the Empire appears very limited. Ireland and the Highlands of Scotland lay outside its borders. The longest river-line of Europe, that of the Rhine and the Danube, was its difficult northern frontier. The Armenian highlands were its fluctuating border on the north-east, in spite of Alexander's deeper penetration, and the survival of Hellenism far into Asia. In the Middle East the sands hemmed it in. Egypt was jealously defended by a system of forts behind the Red Sea coast and the Second Cataract, but Egypt was never more than a strip of green along the Nile. To the west the sands took over to form nature's most defensible frontier, but, at the same time, to confine Roman Africa to the coast and its immediate hinterlands.

Even this dominion was a comparatively recent achievement. Just over a century before Paul reached Rome, Julius Caesar completed that series of eight ruthless campaigns which had crushed the Gauls, and added what is now France and Belgium to the Empire. It was a little longer since Pompey had achieved in the east what his rival Julius Caesar accomplished in the west. By Pompey's conquests and political organization, Asia Minor, Syria, Palestine, all that area of territory which extends from the Dardanelles to the Nile, was knit into the framework of the Empire, which from that date to its final dissolution completely ringed the Mediterranean. Areas were added to Rome after Augustus' death. Britain, up to the wild borders of Scotland, was occupied, and there were major adjustments to the northern and eastern frontiers, but when Christ was born, the city by the Tiber was in sight of the limits of its outward expansion, and it is significant that for many years the conquests of Christianity occupied that very area. Grim though the experience of conquest and alien government was for the peoples of the Mediterranean world, there is no doubt that the unification of that world under the one authority made the initial spread of the Church possible. And it was against the background of the Roman peace that the Church was established and began to play its part in history. Rome provided, in other words, the geographical framework for the story of Acts, and it is worth pausing briefly to examine the historical process by which this situation developed.

Six or seven centuries before Christ a composite community occupied a group of low hills on a strategically advantageous position by the Tiber. It is certain from their language that these people were Italians of the Indo-European stock, that sturdy type which, from 3,000 to 4,000 years ago, drifted out from its central European homelands to fill all Europe, and provide elements in the racial pattern of India, Iran and Asia Minor. The amalgam of tribal elements which formed the settlements by the Tiber is one which archaeologists and ethnologists speculate upon, but which they are still unable to determine. The Romans themselves pictured their first founder Romulus gathering around him a band of refugees, homeless outcasts and fugitives from justice, and stealing their first wives from the Sabines. That legend may indeed suggest a motley origin for the fathers of the Roman race.

There followed the long amazing story of Rome's growth. Strife was the keynote, strife from each experience of which, in the words of one of her own poets,[1] she emerged mightier. Her Etruscan neighbours fell before her, after providing essential

[1] Horace, *Od.* iv. 4. 57–68.

elements in her culture, then little by little the tribes of all Italy, until, by the middle of the third century before Christ, Rome firmly held the long peninsula. Across the sea in Africa was Carthage, and the rich island of Sicily, half Greek, half Carthaginian, lay, a bridgehead and a temptation, between the two continents. The Western Mediterranean, in fact, was not big enough for two major powers. Two great wars were fought, at the end of which Rome found herself with footholds in Africa, in Spain and in Greece.

The search for a stable frontier, which was the central motive of Rome's history, was fairly begun. It was a search which was never completed, but it led step by step, east and west and north, to the imperialism of Christ's day, to a Mediterranean which was a Roman lake, and incidentally to a period of ordered peace which the world had hardly known before, and has not often known since.

Augustus, the first ruler of the system we call the Roman Empire, who steps imperially into the first pages of the story of the New Testament, was a product of the history thus described, and to understand how he came to be the first Roman emperor, the reader must go back 200 years, back in fact to the great wars with Carthage. The Senate ruled Rome in those momentous days, and ruled it well. Theoretically the road to office in that old republic was open to all, by free election, but in actual fact the government tended to fall into the hands of a group of ancient families, who, as the lists show, provided the bulk of Rome's consuls and generals. But Rome had no reason to regret their rule. With dignity and strength in the republic's great centuries this band of born administrators held the stage, and proved a fount of courage and determination on such dark days as those when a Carthaginian army under Hannibal, one of the mighty commanders of all time, ranged through Italy and sat at Rome's very gates. They gave leadership, strength, example and shed their blood with the poorest.

Rome, by force of events, became a world power. It is pointed out above how the search for security against hostile powers in the Mediterranean basin and the Middle East, and against the incalculable irruptions of such hordes of barbarians as came with the Gauls of early Roman history, and the German nomads of one century before Christ, drove Rome to world conquest. The city was called to rule the world, and won almost reluctantly the control of the world, but the machinery of its government proved unequal to the task.

Three unmanageable powers broke the Senate's control. The first was that of the city multitude. The vast devastation of Italy after Hannibal's invasion, and then the economic unbalance which followed conquest and the influx of new wealth, was the first cause of a drift of the agricultural population into the city. In spite of attempts to resettle the people on the land, Rome never solved the problem of her decayed agriculture and her dole-fed mob, the tool and instrument of every political adventurer, a horde with votes to sell, and willing to riot for every demagogue. Law and order in the metropolis deteriorated, and the Senate, weakened by its own growing corruption, proved so unequal to the task of ruling that any observer half a century before Christ might have guessed that some form of autocracy would arise to take its power from the Senate's hands.

The second force which sabotaged the Senate's authority was the irresponsibility of its own members abroad. Men of Rome's ruling class provided the governors for provinces, and the temptations attaching to their office corrupted a generation. Provincials had a right of appeal to the central government and the records of great impeachments survive. They preserve tales of vicious Roman administration in the provinces, and of the bribery, theft, embezzlement, the cruelty, villainy, and greed which accompanied such criminality, almost beyond belief. Such a situation cannot do anything else but damage the institutions and people guilty of its arising. The rulers of Rome, with a few notable exceptions, became cynical, selfish, incompetent, and the prime objects of the moral indignation of the world.

The third disintegrating force was the generals. Distant

provinces with vulnerable frontiers required armies and commanders to lead them. Generals, with armies behind them, bound together, and bound to a popular commander, by the fellowship of arms, conscious of their power, and willing to use it for personal advantage, have ever been a force in history. The Senate in the last century before Christ was at the mercy of its military officers, from Sulla who tried with his army to re-seat the Senate in its position of power, to Julius Caesar who ruthlessly swept it aside, and ruled ably and forcibly as a dictator.

Caesar was assassinated, and out of the tangled politics and civil war which followed his death, rose the man we call Augustus. Augustus was a title of honour conferred in middle life. The man's real name was Octavian, and he was Julius Caesar's adoptive nephew, a mere boy of nineteen when his uncle was murdered, and a student abroad. With singular audacity this remarkable young man travelled to Italy and claimed his inheritance from the dynasts who were striving emulously to lay hold of Rome. By a mixture of good luck and astuteness, a genius for diplomacy, and a deep understanding of men, young Octavian won power, and by his early thirties was undisputed ruler of Rome. The better elements rallied round him, he found able men to win his wars and establish his authority, and the tormented world, which had endured from Rome a century of civil strife and maladministration, saw in Octavian, later called Augustus, the giver of the one thing men desired, peace and security.

Augustus was a clever man. He did not make himself dictator or king. He maintained the fiction that Rome was still a republic. The Senate still met, and he granted it many powers, but he so contrived that power in its essence remained in his own hands. He held various constitutional offices by which the appearance of republican rule was kept up. He retained all the provinces which required the service of armies in his personal control. He appointed virtually all provincial governors, though the Senate in some cases had a harmless hand in the process. The menace of rebellious commanders and civil war was swept away. Corruption disappeared from the provinces. Integrity returned to provincial rule.

It was, then, in a world of unusually stable government and of peace that Christianity first struck root. The words are necessarily used relatively. Behind the line of the Rhine and the Danube the unsolved problems of barbarity remained, and Roman poetry is clear indication[1] that the Empire looked with frequent fear towards the unsettled frontiers over which war might at any time break, and over which, in fact, centuries later, ruinous invasion finally came. But a long era of civil war, the strife of rival claimants to power, the painful days of provincial tyranny, the days of disorder, were finished, and they were ended, as all men saw, by the genius of one man, who while he may, no doubt, have been seeking his own personal advancement, had the wit, nonetheless, to read men's desires aright, and give the stricken world the boon it craved.

The result was a burst of world-wide optimism. The poets of Rome[2] praised Augustus in terms usually reserved for deity, and indeed it was at this time and from this mood that the organized worship of the emperor first became established in the provinces. It was a movement which Rome welcomed as a bond of empire, and although it became the insidious thing which precipitated the clash with the Christian Church, it began in a spontaneous desire with men who were not Romans to show their gratitude towards one who had given a weary world its peace.

Peace was bought with a price. Any semblance of democracy which lingered in the republican constitution of Rome was destroyed under the veiled autocracy which Roman government became. Power, too, as Acton's well-known saying has it, corrupts, and absolute power corrupts absolutely. The saying was illustrated in more than one of Augustus' successors. Recurrent and final tyranny was to make the form and shape of later history.

The provinces, of course, had never known anything but

---

[1] E.g. Horace, *Od.* iii. 29. 25–28; Vergil, *Georg.* i. 498–514.
[2] E.g. Vergil, *Ec.* i. 5; Horace, *Od.* i. 2. 41–52, iii. 5. 2–4; Prop. iv. 6, 37, 38.

despotic rule, and the price of peace was small coin to them; save, perhaps, to the Jews. The valiant struggles whereby, in the era between the Old Testament and the New, they had flung off foreign dominion were still fresh in the mind of history. The books of the Maccabees reveal the heroism and the spirit of that struggle. There is no doubt that the Roman peace was less appreciated in Judaea than elsewhere, and from Judaea, of course, where the worship of a man was abhorrent to a stern and lofty monotheism, came no offer to pay divine honours to any emperor.

Apart, however, from demanding abstention from subversive activity, the docile maintenance of peace, and the steady payment of tribute, the earlier Empire demanded little of her provinces. The time had not yet arrived when loyalty had to be demonstrated by an act of worship before the emperor's statue, and even in those later days such tyranny was only sporadically enforced. Generally speaking Rome was sensible enough to leave untouched as many of the customs and manners of her subjects as she could. The imperial policy towards religion was one of tolerance. The state did, in fact, claim the right, which it had exercised since republican days, to decide what gods might be worshipped, but it did not trouble itself about a man's private opinions, provided he conformed outwardly to a few formal acts of adoration. Even this was not demanded of the Jews, whose religion was early recognized for the stern and exclusive thing it was. Hence Christianity, which was first regarded as a movement within the permitted framework of Judaism, was at first unharmed by state action. The earliest persecution, that of Nero in AD 64, was the personal crime of one in search of handy scapegoats, not the expression of settled policy. It was only twenty years later, in the time of Domitian, that Christianity was recognized as a new force, and a force which, by its very nature and strength, was likely to imperil the state. It was forthwith persecuted.

That clash, which pervades and colours the imagery and theme of the Apocalypse, had not yet developed when Paul preached up and down the Roman world, or indeed when Luke wrote his book. Rome of the Acts of the Apostles is a power which made for peace and opportunity. If Ramsay reads Paul's mind aright, the mighty system fascinated the apostle, and stirred bold thoughts of spiritual conflict. Strife and hostility were to come, but when Paul travelled and Luke wrote, the Empire had not yet become a repressive force. For brief years she policed the world without enmity towards the Church, and the Church used those years well. The Acts of the Apostles is part of the record.

b. The Greeks

The Romans haunt the whole of the New Testament. The Greeks, save possibly for one strange intrusion,[1] have no part in the Gospels, but rise to full view in the Acts of the Apostles. Like the ancestors of the Romans and the Italic tribes, the Greeks, too, came to their Mediterranean peninsula in the days of the great 'folk-wanderings', which brought the Indo-European stock to Europe. The pattern of those wanderings, and their historical extent, has become more and more complex with the discovery, for example, of the nature and significance of the Hittites, and, more recently, with the decipherment of one form of the Cretan script, but such questions of ethnography need not be discussed here.

It is known that civilization was established in the Aegean in the second millennium before Christ, that it died in a dark age of invasion and destruction, and that out of this chaos emerged the complex of peoples on island and mainland which are called the Greeks.

The first centuries of their history, the thinly chronicled and documented centuries in the first half of the pre-Christian millennium, are far from negligible historically. For example, as early as the eighth century before Christ, colonization was spreading Greek ports and trading-posts from the Crimea to Cadiz. It was then that the first fruitful Greek penetration of

[1] Jn. xii. 20–24 (where the Lord's metaphor raises the possibility that the enquirers were Greek nationals, not Hellenistic Jews).

Asia Minor took place. In Ionia, on the Asian side of the Aegean, the foundations of scientific and philosophical thought were laid. On Lesbos, in those same years, Sappho and Alcaeus wrote supreme lyric poetry. In short, the active, inquisitive, brilliant, inventive race of the Greeks was visible in full promise, and known round the eastern Mediterranean coasts, long before its bright flowering in fifth-century Athens.

That flowering is an astonishing phenomenon. In Athens' Golden Age, Greece, or Greece interpreted and made vocal by the dynamic people of Attica, gave immortal gifts to the world. Literature in all its major forms, philosophy and political thought, and plastic art, have been marked, modified, and inspired eternally by what men wrought with hand and mind in one brief noontide of the human spirit, in one amazing city. Everything Greek in all future centuries was deepened and coloured by the achievement of Athens' fifth century. Hellenism, which had centuries of influence still before it, was shaped by Athens, and was to carry the way of life and thought for which it stood to Rome in the west, and the borders of India in the east. In all history there has been nothing quite comparable.

Athens' glory tragically faded, but not before it had passed on essential elements of this strong life and thought. It is not the place here to tell of the great and lamentable war between Athens and the dour and autocratic state of Sparta. It was a conflict of thirty years which bled Athens white, and somehow sapped finally and fatally that vital energy which had made her great achievement. Nor need the next two generations, a sad and sombre epoch for the student of Greek history, be here discussed. They saw the rise of Philip, dictator of Macedon, who overthrew what was left of Greek democracy, and established the autocracy of his highland kingdom on the ruins.

It is more relevant to the theme of Acts to tell of Alexander and one of the most remarkable conquests of history. In the middle of the fourth century before Christ, a remarkable man became king of Macedon. His name was Alexander, and he was the son of Philip, the dictator who had overrun all Greece and established his authority over the whole patchwork of its motley states. Alexander, looking round for tasks to satisfy his restless, questing spirit, and the romanticism born in him from the appeal of Homer's tales of war and valour on the plain of Troy, cast his eyes on Persia. He was certain that the vast Empire, which, a century and a half before, had attacked Europe and brought Greece near to the edge of destruction, was ripe for conquest, and for the bold blow which would shatter in fragments its huge and crumbling structure.

A curious incident lent strength to this conviction. Ten thousand Greek mercenaries in Asia Minor had sold their swords to Cyrus, a local governor, who had raised the standard of revolt against his brother, the King. The army marched on the capital in the plains of Iraq, and in the battle which was fought the Greek troops remained unbeaten, but Cyrus, the rebel, was killed. The victors invited the leaders of the mercenaries to a conference, and treacherously murdered them. In the midst of a great Empire, 600 miles from the sea, 10,000 Greeks were thus marooned without their officers. Bold spirits among them took charge. The army set out, marched north across the rivers, climbed into the mountains of Armenia, fighting its way from valley to valley, range to range, until 6,000 of them reached the Black Sea and took ship for home. Among the survivors was an Athenian named Xenophon who wrote the whole fascinating story in one of literature's most readable books.

Greeks who read the story could only come to one conclusion. An Empire, out of the heart of which a determined band of men could march, was rotten at the core. Alexander proved the deduction correct. He crossed the Dardanelles and took his Macedonians to the plains of the Punjab and the deserts of Libya. When he died at the age of thirty-two, in June 323 BC, the Persian Empire was no more, and the Greeks held the world from their own peninsula to the Indus and the Nile.

When the conqueror succumbed to fever in Babylon, his

generals divided up that world, and out of the division arose the Oriental kingdoms which the Romans conquered two and three centuries later, when their Empire rounded the Mediterranean Sea.

But above and beyond these conquests was a triumph which is peculiarly significant. In the path of Alexander's armies went the Greek language and Greek thought, and out of both emerged the New Testament as we know it. A basic Greek was planted by the armies of Alexander wherever they extended their conquests. In a few generations the entire eastern end of the Mediterranean world was using Greek as a second language and a common vehicle of communication. When the Romans conquered the Greeks in their turn, the Greek language went back to the west with them, and became the common, and to a large extent the spoken language of the Greco-Roman world.

This universal language was waiting to become the vehicle of the Christian message when it began its westward progress. Greek is a marvellously subtle language. Even in its popular form, in which most of the New Testament is written, it is powerful, effective, and most richly expressive. Without the vast flow of the Greek tide eastwards, the New Testament could not have been born. Greek provided its language, and Greek provided its fashion of thought. Part of the influence of Hellenism, which somehow accompanied the Greek language, was a stimulus to the human mind. To reason, to question, to speculate, was a habit of the Greeks. To ask why, and to endeavour to answer the query, was their preoccupation. Such fashions of thinking moulded Greek culture, and it was in contact with Greek culture, in Tarsus of Cilicia, that Paul acquired his habit of logical thought as well as the language which formed its vehicle.

Paul's part in interpreting the Christian faith to the Greek world is the major theme of the Acts of the Apostles. Without a Greek education, as Luke's story will abundantly illustrate, Paul could not have compassed this task. Nor could he have been the versatile genius whom the reader of Luke's vivid pages meets and learns to appreciate, nor indeed the personality which stands life-size behind his own powerful writings.

Added, of course, to the culture of Greece, was that of Palestine, absorbed at its best at Gamaliel's feet. Paul's theory of revelation, and his synthesis of the covenants, so inspired and so compelling in its logic, was the work of a Greek Jew. It was thought trained in the Hellenism of Tarsus which solved the problem of the Testaments, and brought from out of the stores of Judaism the wares which Christians could recognize and use. And since the modern world is the heir of three civilizations, passed on, synthetized and harmonized by the Christian Church, there is a sense in which Paul was the first European.

The Empire of Rome was an empire of law, authority and political power. But Greece, as a Roman poet[1] had himself observed, had long since 'led captive her fierce conqueror'. The Greek empire of the mind was a reality to be felt in all the lands of Paul and the Acts of the Apostles. Rome prepared the geographical stage for the new faith, the Greeks prepared the intellectual scene.

Of the Greeks themselves a few are met in the story, betraying all the faults and excellencies of their race. In the brief and vivid narrative of Paul at Athens, the reader of Acts is taken to the queen city of the Greeks in the late Indian Summer of her greatness. The picture is sharp and clear. Sophisticated, supercilious, intellectually arrogant, and living on, if not in, a cultural past, the philosophers of two schools reject the Christian message. At Thessalonica, Philippi, Corinth and Ephesus the Greeks appear again in their varied guise, factious, emotional, clever and questing, a people as they always were to stir in turn admiration and exasperation. Paul knew them, and moved among them easily. If what he said was to some Greeks 'foolishness',[2] there were others who formed the fabric of his Church.

[1] Horace, *Ep.* ii. 1. 156.
[2] 1 Cor. i. 23.

31

c. *The Jews and the Religious Situation in Palestine*

(*i*) *Abraham's descendants.* The dates are not certainly established, but it must have been some thirteen centuries before Christ when nomad tribes broke out of the eastern wilderness across the Jordan, and began the conquest of Palestine. In Europe the racial pattern of the great Indo-European folk-wandering was taking shape, but the Hebrew movement into Palestine had nothing in common with this. The tribes came fresh from Egyptian domination back to a land which their ancestors had known. They came welded by tyranny and desert living into a strong and dynamic people. They came with their national consciousness sharpened and solemnized by the recent memory of a great deliverance.

Nomad living was not new to their history. Their remoter ancestors had left Ur of the Chaldees at the head of the Persian Gulf, and followed the old caravan routes which led from that ancient centre of human culture up the Euphrates Valley and round the curve of the Fertile Crescent. The mounds of ruin which mark the site of Ur stand today 150 miles from the sea, but in Abraham's day the waters where men first learned navigation extended to her neighbourhood, and Ur was not only the centre of a rich alluvial plain but a nodal point of trade and travel. Her pottery has been found at Mohenjo-Daro on the Indus and her ships no doubt sought the Tamil coast and Ceylon. Abraham, whose name has been mentioned, was one of the most significant figures of ancient history, and it is curious to note how the perennial conspiracy of history and geography placed his birth and breeding at a place as significant as Ur. It will be shown in these pages how Tarsus was the one place in a later world where Paul could have received the education and outlook which made him what he was for the infinite blessing of man. So with the Paul of the Old Testament; Ur, at the head of the Persian Gulf, was the one place in the early years of the second millennium before Christ, where a man could fruitfully apprehend the world of east and west as Abraham must have apprehended it.

And the spectacle of that vast world, its problems, its darkness, and its need, must have been the background of Abraham's call to found a nation under God.

'The God of glory', said Stephen (vii. 2), 'appeared unto our father Abraham, when he was in Mesopotamia.' Abraham had grasped a grand and vital truth, that God was one and beside Him was no other, and that man came to such a God by faith. So it was that Abraham was called to abandon the city of the moon-goddess. He set out to establish a people in another land, a nation which should differ from all other nations, and through whom all the tribes of earth should be blessed. Such is the difference which sacred history must note, as it watches the desert tribes moving across the Jordan. They were bound and inspired by a sense of destiny unknown to the war-bands which filtered down the Balkan peninsula to form the Greek peoples, or who colonized the long Italian peninsula by road and sea-way. Ignorant, fierce, vicious, the Hebrews could be, but they were never without devoted spirits who held and cherished some remnant of an ancient vision, and saw in their people's future a task, a purpose, and a calling which set them apart.

Abraham's camp had become a people, disciplined and hardened by oppression, and trained in the uprooted nomadry of the Sinai wilderness. And amid the stress of the latter experience they had received a code which, through all their subsequent history, they called 'the Law'. Viewed in the record, and outside the context of events which had attended its giving, the Law, save in one point, was not unique. Earlier peoples had codified the social obligations of man to man. In the Euphrates Valley and on the Syrian coast, men earlier in time had made wise provisions for justice, order, and the regulation of life, and recorded the same for all to read. But the Law, as it came to the Hebrew people from the inspired hand of Moses, their amazing leader, was a code theocratically conceived, a code with a ritual and a symbolism implicit and attached which did more than impose an order of righteousness on a primitive people.

A spiritual message was interfused, and those who knew, practised and understood the Law of Israel, were made in the act aware of deeper truths, taught to associate the ideas of sin and death, to realize the utter holiness of God, that the most High is not to be approached by the unclean and the defiled, that He redeems, indeed will redeem, preserves, guides and sanctifies. They learned, too, from the elaborate Tent of the Witness that God is not visible, nor to be shaped and represented by clumsy human hands, but that nevertheless He dwelt amid His own to bless and to keep.

Through the vicissitudes of the nation's history as it was out-worked on the little stage of Palestine for the next fourteen centuries, the best and most devoted minds of the people clung triumphantly to these thoughts. There were those at all times to whom the Law was so much imposed obligation, an exercise to perform, a mechanical system by which man appeased an angry and offended God. There were those for many centuries who caught the spirit of surrounding paganism, and 'went after' strange gods, and found base satisfaction in the idolatries and obscenities of pagan cults.

But the 'remnant' of those who saw profounder truth, who grasped vital fragments of a great historic plan, and who saw the significance of God's doings with their race, was never utterly lost to view in the record of the Old Testament. Hence the prophets, who were frequently misunderstood, often persecuted, sometimes martyred by their own folk. Their recorded words are Israel's great contribution to human thought in days when Israel's own existence was daily menaced by such military systems as those of Assyria and Babylon, and when one season's capricious aggression might have seen the little nation follow others into oblivion.

Geography and history conspired again. There is an eloquent passage by George Adam Smith[1] on the subject: 'There is no land', writes the geographer, 'which is so much a sanctuary and an observatory as Palestine: no land which, till its office was fulfilled, was so swept by the great forces of history,

[1] *The Historical Geography of the Holy Land*, pp. 112 f.

and yet so capable of preserving one tribe in national continuity and growth: one tribe learning and suffering and rising superior to the successive problems these forces presented to her, till upon the opportunity afforded by the last of them she launched with her results upon the world. . . . If a man can believe there is no directing hand behind our universe and the history of our race, he will, of course, say that all this is the result of chance. But for most of us only another conclusion is possible.'

(*ii*) *Israel between the Testaments.* How, therefore, did the tragic elements of the New Testament story emerge? Those who move before the reader in the company of Christ, or who appear in the Acts of the Apostles as the first bearers of His word, are in the lineal descent of those who, as Stephen showed in his brilliant address to the Sanhedrin, had kept the first faith and the vision undimmed. Ranged against them in the New Testament and in the Old were those who misconceived and perverted the truth. Arid days lay between the Testaments, days in which, after the fashion of man's dealing with divine things, spirit had been lost in letter, and institutions had atrophied and died. The Law, the education of Israel, the 'schoolmaster' to lead to Christ, had lost its purpose and become an end in itself. Save for John, suddenly appearing to stir and to disturb, and to link a brief and fiery career with the story of the New Testament, the voice of prophecy had been silent for four centuries when Christ was born in Roman-occupied Palestine. Religion had become, in the hands of its exponents, a barren province of legal exercise and sophistry. The zeal which had salutarily preserved the Law through days of grim exile and disaster had turned cancerous and was multiplying its activity without meaning. For others religion had become not a blessed experience to propagate and preach to hungry and dependent multitudes, but a vested interest and a source of gain. To understand the Gospels, to understand the Acts of the Apostles and the whole New Testament, it is most vitally necessary to apprehend the religious situation in

Palestine, the backslidden state of Israel at large, the retreat of religion to the few and the despised, the great betrayal of the Sadducees, and the mortal disease of the spirit which afflicted those who were called 'the scribes and the Pharisees'.

(iii) *The Pharisees*. Judaism, as expounded by the scribes and the Pharisees, was the first great enemy of the Church, as it had been the mortal foe of the Lord Himself. Who were these Pharisees, who move through page after page of the New Testament as the champions of a monumental tradition, the bitter foes of innovation, casuists and formalists at the best, but at the worst the veriest of hypocrites, and a by-word for sham and pretence where such vices are most reprehensible? Thanks to their record in the New Testament, the term Pharisee has passed into the languages of the world as a generic term for those who cherish 'pretensions to superior sanctity . . . self-righteous persons, formalists, hypocrites'.[1] It is important, however, to penetrate beyond this derived significance, and to form a clear idea of what the Pharisees really were, what they stood for and why they played the part they did.

It should be remembered that the Pharisees were once a great people. Nor had such nobility quite vanished; Nicodemus and Gamaliel, who make brief and dignified appearances in the New Testament, give some indication of what Pharisees could be, and what they once perhaps predominantly were. The Pharisees were a kind of guild or society, comprising both rabbis and laymen. The word 'Pharisee' means 'separated', and was adopted by the group because they regarded themselves as 'cut off' from the rest of Jewry in important ways, by deeper sanctity, a closer regard for the Law, and stricter habits of eating. The order, if we may call it such, came into being about a century and a half before the birth of Christ, and, if Josephus is correct, never numbered more than about 6,000 members. Its chief aim in the early days of its activity was to preserve the Jews and their unique heritage from

[1] *Oxford English Dictionary*. Also see *Oxford Dictionary of Quotations*.

36

foreign contagion in general, and from the corrupting influence, first of the Greeks and then of the Romans, in particular. At first these high pretensions did much good. The seductive power of Greek thought was stemmed at a time when its tendency to scepticism might have contaminated Judaism disastrously. The Pharisees, too, must in general have interpreted their profession convincingly in upright living and exemplary conduct, for their fraternity in its early days secured a reputation for righteousness with the common people, and it was a proverbial saying that if but two persons entered heaven, one of them would be a Pharisee. They played a great part in purifying Judaism and it is a significant fact that idolatry, against which the Old Testament wages unremitting war to the end of its record, had ceased to be an issue by New Testament times. The credit for this victory undoubtedly goes to the Pharisees.

But, as so often happens in the institutions of men, sincerity gave place to formalism, and zeal for the Law became a passion for rigid legality. The Pharisees believed that Moses had received, along with the written Law, an oral law which was preserved in the traditions of men. These traditions they set out to elaborate and extend. A voluminous literature grew up of rulings, instances and examples, by which the Pharisees built up a corpus of legislation until it became the burden of which Christ Himself complained (Mt. xxiii. 4).

The charge may perhaps be best illustrated from the laws and regulations with which the Pharisees surrounded the Sabbath. 'Of all their sacred institutions', writes David Smith, 'there was none which the Jews regarded with such veneration as the Sabbath.'[1] Indeed, within the context of its original foundation, there was none more worthy of preservation. The Law in its essential humanity had laid it down that every seventh day should be given over to the refreshment of mind and body, and this beneficent ordinance the Rabbis turned into a grievous bondage. They amplified and applied the Mosaic enactment with disastrous ingenuity. On the Sabbath, said the

[1] *The Days of his Flesh*, pp. 131 ff., where authorities are collected.

commandment, 'thou shalt do no work'. The scribes drew up a list of forty works save one which were forbidden and which, if done knowingly, rendered the offender liable to stoning, and if done inadvertently demanded a heavy sin-offering in expiation. These thirty-nine works in the technical language of the legalists were called 'fathers', and the subsections of derivative pieces of labour were called 'descendants'.

Ploughing was a 'father', digging a 'descendant', but to dig on the Sabbath did not require a spade and deliberate delving. For instance, it was forbidden to drag a chair along the ground in case it should score the surface; and although it was permitted to expectorate on a hard pavement and remedy the lack of hygiene by a rub of the foot, it was a debatable point whether one might do the same on the bare ground, lest the action disturb the surface, and become technically ploughing. Another of the 'fathers' was carrying a load, and this had a host of 'descendants'. To walk with a crutch or a wooden leg was allowed, but not on stilts, because stilts were carried, and did not carry the man. To wear a superfluous garment was to carry a burden. The tailor was required to leave his needle and thread at home on Friday towards sunset, and the scribe his pen, lest the Sabbath overtake them abroad with burdens. A weighty question under this head arose if a man's house caught fire on the Sabbath. Was he permitted to rescue anything? Nothing, if it involved carrying; but there was a way out with regard to the salvage of clothing. A garment necessary for warmth or respectability could be put on, and the wearer could then proceed outside and deposit it in a place of safety. Then, returning to the house, he could rescue another article of clothing in similar fashion, and so on, fire and ruin permitting, until the whole wardrobe was safely outside. Another 'father' work was reaping, and this, as is illustrated by the action of the disciples in the corn-field, included pulling an ear or blade. A woman was forbidden to look in the mirror on the Sabbath lest she should see a grey hair and be tempted to pluck it out.

These are but a few instances of the clutter of nonsense with which the scribes and Pharisees had surrounded one institution only of the Law. The worst feature of it was that, when the mass of legislation proved impossible of performance, casuistic subterfuges were devised by the same legal experts, as means of escape by which they and others could circumvent their own regulations. A most useful fiction was what was called 'connections'. A Sabbath-day's journey was 2,000 cubits beyond the city; but suppose a man wish' d to go farther than that on the Sabbath. On Friday he could travel to the boundary and deposit food for two meals. This point then technically became his home, and on the Sabbath he could travel to it, and then continue as far again. Or, to quote another example, it was unlawful on the Sabbath day to carry anything from one house to another. But suppose several houses looked on to one square or courtyard. The various inhabitants had only to deposit a little food here on Friday, and the whole area was considered as one house on the Sabbath, with all the neighbours able to go and come with what they desired. Another effectual method devised by the lawyers for evading their own Sabbath-observance regulations was that known as 'intention'. For example, it was not lawful to eat an egg which a fowl had thoughtlessly laid on the Sabbath day. But if one stated beforehand that the hen was intended for the table, the egg might be legitimately eaten, as being something which had merely fallen off the doomed hen.

This Rabbinical passion for the letter of the Law had more serious implications. It vitiated the whole religious outlook. There was not an event or action in the daily life of the orthodox Jew in the Pharisaic caste which was not in some fashion under the bondage of a formal legalism. At every step, at his work, at meals, at home, abroad, from morning till night, from youth till age, the zealous Pharisee was faced with dead and deadening formulae. A healthy moral life flagged and withered under such a burden. And this indeed accounted for some of the stories told of the Pharisees: of the Rabbis Gidal and Jochanan, for example, who, when rebuked for their pastime of sitting in the women's bathing-place, replied that they were of the lineage of Joseph, over whom sin had no dominion. The Law, as it was enforced and interpreted by the stricter Pharisees, was a force destructive of moral freedom and ultimately a menace to morality itself. Hence the vast gap which had opened between the religious leaders and the community. The common man knew he could not possibly keep the Law as his leaders interpreted it. Indeed many of its artificial extensions and consequential escape clauses were unknown to any but the experts. The result was that the common man threw out good and bad together, made a show of doing what he was told, but gained little comfort or spiritual aid from those who were supposed to minister divine things to him; in short, like a hungry sheep, in the famous phrase, he 'looked up and was not fed'. The Pharisees, proud of their artificial sanctity, and self-righteous, with texts from the Law elegantly written and dangling from forehead and arms, looked down with contempt on those whose spiritual wellbeing should have been their first responsibility. 'This multitude which knoweth not the law', sneered the Jerusalem hierarchy, 'is accursed.'

(iv) *The Sadducees.* Opposed to the Pharisees was the politico-religious sect or society of the Sadducees. The name appears to derive from the high priest Zadok (2 Sa. viii. 17). The party originated in the days of the Hasmoneans, and bore the colours of its worldly origin. In the days of the Acts, as in the time of Christ, it held such power as the Romans in their canny imperialism left to be exercised by subject peoples. The Sadducees were collaborators, and the opponents of religious strictness. They repudiated the oral tradition on which the Pharisees had made their mountain of burdensome legislation, and accepted only the written Law. They rejected doctrines of retribution, resurrection and immortality, and in consequence all belief in angels or spirits. Their hostility, first to the Lord and then to the Church, was due to their careful policy of collaboration with the occupying power, and consequent dislike of popular movements or disturbing political events. If

Pharisaism led to a breakdown of morality under the sheer burden of formalism, the beliefs and preoccupations of the Sadducees provided little basis at all for morality, and encouraged cynicism, place-seeking and materialism. They made the temple 'a den of thieves', removed Christ in the interests of expediency, and represent in their ancient setting the worst vices of hierarchy and corrupt religion.

(*v*) *The true Israel.* Had Judaism been confined to these two testimonies, there would have been no link of life between the preparation and the fulfilment. There is evidence, however, of a stronger and purer tradition out of which came the expectation, the outreaching faith, and the yearning for redemption, which gave the Lord His contact with human hearts, and recruited the first disciples of the Church. There were other Jews than scribes, high priests and Pharisees.

The early chapters of Luke's Gospel introduce us to men like Zacharias the priest, and Elizabeth his wife, to Simeon and Anna, not to mention Mary herself. John gives us a glimpse of the eager disciples of the Baptist, and Nathanael, the 'Israelite indeed'. The old clean sources of the Jewish faith had not been choked. We can trace them back to Amos and Elijah. Religion, entrenched and codified, adapted comfortably to the whims of rulers and modified to suit the needs of vested interests, was never safe from the prophet of the desert, the attack and onslaught of some godly commoner with the pure zeal of God alive in his heart, and God's word on his lips.

Such a one was John the Baptist, the son of a humble priest, but untrained in the Pharisaic schools, and unsupported by Sadducean power. It has been suggested that John drew training and inspiration from the Essenes. Hard by the scenes of his ministry, these desert anchorites had their abodes. Turning, like Abraham, from the corruptions of city life, these worthy folk spent their days in toil, prayer and fasting. Their influence was vast. Even Josephus, future historian of the Jews, spent three years in one of their communities. In the preparation for the gospel, the Essenes played a part.

The Dead Sea Scrolls, first discovered in 1947, have thrown vivid light on this stream of Jewish religious life. The sect which lived in the Qumran Monastery, and whose libraries, hidden in caves, are the now famous scrolls, were not themselves Essenes. In the story of their religious community, however, as the archaeologists piece it together, we gain another glimpse into those purer groups of Jewry from which the first disciples of Christ were recruited, and who formed the rank and file of the first Christian Church.

Whatever the Church may at subsequent times have become, it had its deep roots in the common people of Palestine. By the official leaders of religion it was despised and persecuted, to maintain intact the policy of collaboration with Rome (Jn. xi. 48), and to preserve unbroken such profitable monopolies as that which the Lord drove briefly from the temple.

d. The Jews of the Dispersion

There is another aspect of ancient Jewry, no less vital to the story of Acts, of which the records are less clear and ready to hand. They are scattered abroad, written in the papyrus records of some Nile-side town, in some epitaph or inscription which tells an archaeologist of a Jewish grave or synagogue, in an imperial decree, a sentence from Suetonius, or a scornful line from a Roman satirist, and the hundred odd corners where historians find the raw material of history.

Whence arose the network of Jewish communities throughout the world? Some perhaps followed trade. The age-old communities of Jews in the Yemen and in India are, perhaps, the descendants of those who represented Solomon in the days of the partnership with Tyre, when the 'ships of Tarshish' traded out of Ezion-geber on the Gulf of Akaba. Others were deportees. Assyria and Babylon weakened their subjects and strengthened their homeland by mass deportation. In 1909 the papyrus records of a Jewish colony were discovered at Aswan. They were mercenaries of Persia guarding the Nubian frontier. The book of Esther is a document of the Jewish remnant at Susa; the book of Daniel is the brave record of the Jews of Babylon. In Alexandria, where three-fifths of a vast city were Jews, the Septuagint, Greek translation of the Old Testament, is a worthy monument to faith and zeal. Tarsus had a Jewish aristocracy of Roman citizens, and Paul found synagogues from Cyprus to Greece and Rome. The story of Pentecost lists sixteen peoples whose Jewish members were present in Jerusalem for the Passover.

These colonies were kept separate and distinct by the cohesive power of the Jewish faith. In these foreign fields the literal observance of the Mosaic Law was difficult, and this may be the reason why the Jews of the Dispersion were saved from the legalism of metropolitan Jewry, and obtained a truer insight into the spiritual meaning of the Old Testament. Like Simon of Cyrene, the Jews of the Dispersion came up to Jerusalem like Moslems to Mecca, for the great festivals of the faith, and for the religious pilgrimage they each sought most passionately to make, but it was impossible for them to remain unaffected by the atmosphere of their adopted lands. They learned, perforce, the language of the community in which they dwelt, and all unconsciously imbibed their ideas and acquired their manners.

The proud Judaeans tended to look down on such poorer brethren. They wonder scornfully in the Gospel story whether Jesus will 'go to the Dispersion among the Gentiles and teach the Gentiles' (see Jn. vii. 35). They speak of this 'accursed crowd which knows not the Law' (see Jn. vii. 49). But such life as Judaism possessed, had they but known it, was rather among the Jews of the Dispersion than in its homeland. Jerusalem Jewry was dead of its own atrophied outlook, its paralysis of legalism, and the malady of its pride. Abroad were such men as Apollos, Stephen, Philip and Paul.

The Dispersion, in the purposes of God, provided, first, stepping-stones for the gospel. Paul's method, based on his sound view of God's plan, was to begin with the synagogue, and build upon its congregation's knowledge of the Old Testament. Contrast his methods with the Greek philosophers at Athens, where he went back for a foundation to universal theism. But the significant fact is that he seldom failed to find Jews to begin his mission. Most of Paul's letters quite clearly assume Old Testament backgrounds and at least a Jewish element in the congregation addressed. Thus, throughout the world, the biblical link of Old and New Testament was retained. The response varied, but the part played by the Jews of the Dispersion in the propagation of the gospel cannot be over-emphasized.

Secondly, for completeness of conclusion, another point should be reiterated. Before the chill of Pharisaism settled on his mind, Paul's outlook was broadened and spiritualized by contact with the Greeks. Ramsay quotes aptly the testimony of 'two of the most learned Jews of modern times'. These men denied that Paul could have written the letters attributed to him 'because there is much in them which no Jew could write'. These men, says Ramsay, 'knew old Jewish feeling with an intimacy no Western scholar can ever attain to. They appreciated the non-Jewish element mingled with the writings of Paul. They rightly recognized that no mere Jew could write like that; but instead of inferring that Paul was more than a mere Jew in education and mind, they argued that he, being a pure and narrow Jew, could not have written the letters.'

Thus the three streams of God's historical preparation for the gospel converge in Paul, the son of Tarsus and Jerusalem. The man of twin cultures, bilingual and cosmopolitan, the Roman citizen, interpreter of Christ to Jews and Greeks, disputer of the synagogue, orator of the philosopher's assembly, Old Testament scholar, and writer of one-quarter of the New.[1]

---

[1] *The Teaching of Paul in Terms of the Present Day*, v and vi. *The Cities of Saint Paul*, i, iv and v.

ANALYSIS

I. THE COMMISSION AND THE ENABLEMENT (i. 1–ii. 13).

    a. The prologue (i. 1, 2).
    b. The resurrection ministry (i. 3–8).
    c. The ascension (i. 9–11).
    d. At Jerusalem (i. 12–26).
    e. Pentecost (ii. 1–13).

II. THE CHURCH IN ACTION (ii. 14–iv. 31).

    a. Peter's first sermon (ii. 14–40).
    b. First rapture (ii. 41–47).
    c. At the Beautiful Gate (iii. 1–11).
    d. Peter's second sermon (iii. 12–26).
    e. The Sadducean persecution (iv. 1–7).
    f. Peter's third sermon (iv. 8–12).
    g. Conflict (iv. 13–31).

III. 'MID TOIL AND TRIBULATION (iv. 32–v. 42).

    a. The Church in unity (iv. 32–37).
    b. The Church divided (v. 1–11).
    c. The second persecution (v. 12–26).
    d. In the Sanhedrin (v. 27–42).

IV. THE HELLENISTIC JEWS (vi. 1–viii. 40).

    a. The deacons (vi. 1–7).
    b. Stephen's ministry (vi. 8–15).
    c. Stephen's speech (vii. 1–53).
    d. Stephen's martyrdom (vii. 54–viii. 4).
    e. Philip's ministry (viii. 5–40).

V. THE DAMASCUS ROAD (ix. 1–31).

    a. The man (ix. 1, 2).
    b. The conversion (ix. 3–9).
    c. The sequel (ix. 10–31).

ACTS OF THE APOSTLES

VI. PETER USES THE KEYS (ix. 32–xii. 25).

  a. Lydda (ix. 32–35).
  b. Joppa (ix. 36–x. 23).
  c. Caesarea (x. 24–48).
  d. Jerusalem (xi. 1–18).
  e. The wider world (xi. 19–30).
  f. Jerusalem again (xii. 1–19).
  g. Caesarea again (xii. 20–25).

VII. THE FIRST JOURNEY (xiii. 1–xiv. 26).

  a. Antioch (xiii. 1–3).
  b. Cyprus (xiii. 4–12).
  c. Perga (xiii. 13).
  d. Antioch in Pisidia (xiii. 14–50).
  e. Iconium (xiii. 51–xiv. 5).
  f. Lystra (xiv. 6–19).
  g. Derbe (xiv. 20, 21a).
  h. Back to Syrian Antioch (xiv. 21b–26).

VIII. THE JERUSALEM CONFERENCE (xiv. 27–xv. 35).

  a. Report at Antioch (xiv. 27–xv. 3).
  b. Discussion at Jerusalem (xv. 4–29).
  c. The application of the decree (xv. 30, 31).
  d. The unfolding plan (xv. 32–35).

IX. INTO EUROPE (xv. 36–xvii. 14).

  a. Antioch again (xv. 36–39).
  b. Syria and Cilicia (xv. 40, 41).
  c. Galatia again (xvi. 1–5).
  d. Asia (xvi. 6–8).
  e. Troas (xvi. 9–11).
  f. Philippi (xvi. 12).
  g. The gospel in Europe (xvi. 13–40).
  h. Thessalonica (xvii. 1–9).
  i. Berea (xvii. 10–14).

X. ATHENS (xvii. 15–34).

  a. The visitor (xvii. 15–17).
  b. The audience (xvii. 18–21).
  c. The sermon (xvii. 22–31).
  d. The sequel (xvii. 32–34).

46

COMMENTARY

I. THE COMMISSION AND THE ENABLEMENT
(i. 1–ii. 13)

a. The prologue (i. 1, 2)

The book is a sequel, and it is more than likely that Luke had a third volume in view. It was practicable to make papyrus rolls to about 35 feet in length, and the units of a writer's work tended to be determined by this limitation. Luke has used his space with some skill. His two rolls have given us the two longest books in the New Testament.

It is reasonable to suppose that *Theophilus* (1) was a real person. Nothing is known of him. He was certainly not Seneca, as one rash conjecture would have it. It is impossible to decide whether he was Jew or Greek, or whether the omission of the honourable title employed in the Gospel (Lk. i. 3) indicates a deepening of friendship, the abandonment of office, or conversion to Christianity. All these matters have been the subject of not very profitable debate. The language of verse 1 suggests that Christ's work did not end with His earthly ministry. Through the Holy Spirit and His Church He continues from heaven what He commenced on earth.

b. The resurrection ministry (i. 3–8)

The fact of the resurrection was to be the solid foundation of the apostles' faith and the chief ingredient of their early message. The transformation in the disciples of Christ, evident to anyone who reads the closing chapters of the Gospels and the opening chapters of Acts, is itself justification for the adjective *infallible* (3) employed in the AV to extract the full flavour of the one noun used in the Greek text.

Some have imagined contradictions here with Lk. xxiv. 49–52. It is obvious that the writer saw none, nor in fact do they exist. The Gospel does not mention, but does not preclude, the forty days. Bethany and the Mount of Olives are topographically identical. The reported words are substantially the same.[1]

For *the promise of the Father* (4) see Joel ii. 28–32; Lk. xxiv. 49; Jn. xiv. 16, 26, xv. 26. It was a function of the promised Holy Spirit to enlarge the understanding of spiritual truth, and verses 6 and 7 are not without relevance to verse 5. Here were the same bewildered men, still bound in mind and spirit by those narrow conceptions of the purposes of God which had dogged them in the days of their Master's earthly ministry. Consider, too, that Luke reports this brief conversation and rebuke with the future unfolding of his theme in mind. It was a very different notion of 'the kingdom' which was to find expression in the work of Paul, and which Luke had in mind to describe. 'The change from the spirit which dictated the question in the verse (6), to that in which Peter (ii. 38, 39) preached repentance and forgiveness to all whom the Lord should call, is one of the greatest evidences of the miracle of Pentecost.'[2]

The widening circles of verse 8 reflect the development of the theme in the book, but such geographical development does not determine the plan of Luke's narrative. Verses 6 and 7 are more significant in that regard. Luke's theme rather moves to Paul's global and imperial conception of the gospel. It necessarily moves in widening geographical orbits. But the principle expressed in verse 8 has an evangelistic application at all times. To press outward from the fringe is always sound policy, provided it is done with vigour and devotion.

c. The ascension (i. 9–11)

It is perhaps necessary to remark that the modern mind,

---

[1] J. R. Lumby (*Cambridge Greek Testament*, p. 82) deals in detail with the questions; also R. J. Knowling in the *Expositor's Greek Testament*, II, pp. 70 f.
[2] J. R. Lumby, *op. cit.*, p. 83.

bemused a little by its materialistic conception of the sum of things, has found difficulty in this story. C. S. Lewis deals well with the subject.[1] 'What troubles us here', he concludes, 'is not simply the statement itself but what (we feel sure) the author meant by it. Granted that there are different natures, different levels of being, distinct but always discontinuous— granted that Christ withdrew from one of these into another . . . what precisely should we expect the onlookers to see? Perhaps mere instantaneous vanishing would make us feel most comfortable. A sudden break between the perceptible and the imperceptible would worry us less than any kind of joint. But if the spectators say they saw first a short vertical movement and then a vague luminosity (that is what "cloud" presumably means here as it certainly does in the account of the Transfiguration) and then nothing—have we any reason to object?' In other words, some of the difficulty encountered arises from an over-literal interpretation of the words. Those who told the story sought to narrate, in simple and intelligible words, an astonishing and an overwhelming experience. Christ passed into a world beyond human comprehension, and language can only speak of that world in symbols of wealth, royalty and elevation.

The miracle, of course, remains, and the historian cannot be divided. There have been those who have granted a large measure of historiographical merit to the Luke of the later chapters, who have yet felt put out by the same historian's frank acceptance of miracle at the beginning of the story. But we have one historian, not two, in both the Gospel and the book before us. Some words may be quoted from Sir William Ramsay's final testimony to our author: 'It became more and more clear that it is impossible to divide Luke's history into parts, attributing to one portion the highest authority as the first-hand narrative of a competent and original authority, while regarding the rest as of quite inferior mould. . . . The history must stand as a whole and be judged as a whole. If one part shows striking historical excellence, so must all; if any

[1] *Miracles*, pp. 177 ff. *Cit.*, p. 186.

part shows a conspicuous historical blunder, we must be very suspicious of a theory which attributes surpassing qualities to another part.'[1]

The promise of the return (11) must be similarly emancipated from the inadequacies of human speech. The angelic visitants did not mean that the Lord would emerge from 'a cloud' in downward motion, but that at a point of time and place, He would again break from that other world into this, out of eternity into time and history.

d. At Jerusalem (i. 12-26)

In verse 13 the definite article should be read. They went to *the* upper room, probably the scene of the Supper (Mk. xiv. 15; Lk. xxii. 12). This would seem to them the logical place to await the promise (4), a place of sacred and awesome memories, and the likeliest scene of a visitation they could not envisage, but which filled them with tense expectation.

They were all there save Judas, and Luke no doubt lists the names to set on record the fact that all were in place again, the panic past, and loyalty reborn. His book, moreover, is to single out but one or two of the band for mention, and then to show another, not yet called, moving to the fore and dominating the scene. It is appropriate that this initial tribute should be paid. The adverb translated *with one accord* (14) (cf. also ii. 1) stresses a prerequisite of effectiveness too often forgotten in our divided Christendom. Knowling points out[2] that the adverb is used by Luke in this book ten or eleven times, and once only elsewhere in the New Testament (Rom. xv. 6). *The women* (14) also were present. 'Time after time', writes Ramsay on this verse, 'Luke is our only authority for the service and ministration of women. He had the tender and sympathetic feeling for women which seems to be quite in keeping with his surroundings in Macedonia (where women

[1] *Was Christ Born at Bethlehem?* pp. 36 f.
[2] *Op. cit.*, p. 61.

occupied a place of so much more honour than in Greece proper).'[1]

In the four evangelists there is discernible a consistency of characterization which sets a strong mark of authenticity on the narratives. Peter ever craved for action in times of tension (e.g. Jn. xx. 3, xxi. 3), and usually persuaded others to follow his bold lead. Here (15) he runs true to form. His citation of Old Testament authority is natural argument for one who habitually thought in the forms, language and imagery of the Scriptures, and the speech is highly consistent with Peter's later manner as recorded in the narrative, and with his own writings.

The account of Judas' fate (18–20) is not inconsistent with that set forth by Matthew (xxvii. 3–10). The field was probably bought by the legally-minded priests in Judas' name. Amid the crazed inconsistencies of despair he may have laid claim to it in consequence, and in bitter irony made it the scene of suicide. The two accounts preserve different but equally true details from the rest of the shocking story, and the field won its sombre name on more than one count.

We hear no more of the good Matthias (23–26) save for the legend of Ethiopian martyrdom, and it is commonly assumed that Peter ran ahead of God's purpose in seeking this appointment. Paul was destined for the vacant place. The casting of lots was a provision of the Law (Lv. xvi. 8), and as such a practice of immaturity. Chrysostom was the first to note that these events took place before Pentecost. The Spirit of truth made such actions obsolete.

e. Pentecost (ii. 1–13)

The institution of the harvest festival, fifty days after the presentation of the 'wave-sheaf' in the passover week, is described in Lv. xxiii. 15–21. Imagination has ranged so widely and extravagantly in 'typological' interpretations of the Old Testament that modern orthodox scholarship rightly treats the

[1] *Op. cit.*, p. 90 (Lk. vii. 36 ff., viii. 2, x. 38, xi. 27, xxiii. 27, 29, 55).

subject with some reserve. It is not, however, unreasonable to see the visitation of this chapter as a fulfilment. 'Was this feast also,' asks S. H. Kellogg, 'like the passover, prophetic? The New Testament is scarcely less clear than in the former case. For after that Christ, first having been slain as "our Passover", had then risen from the dead as the "firstfruits", fulfilling the type of the wave-sheaf on the morning of the Sabbath, fifty days passed; "and when the day of Pentecost was fully come", came that great outpouring of the Holy Ghost . . . and the formation of that Church of the New Testament, whose members the Apostle James declares (i. 18) to be a kind of firstfruits of God's creatures.'[1] It is evident that those who habitually thought in the forms and imagery of the Old Testament saw this correspondence between ritual and history. It further follows that, since the choice of the day was a sovereign act of God, the interpretation is divinely sanctioned.

The language of verses 2 and 3 seeks to reduce to simple and intelligible terms an unearthly and indescribable experience. Luke faced a similar difficulty in describing the Lord's ascension (i. 9, 10), and the reserve evident in both narratives is the measure of his regard for truth. F. J. Foakes-Jackson[2] is quite astray in alleging a certain preoccupation with dramatic and vivid narration in these and similar contexts, where Luke does not write as an eyewitness. We 'sons to Aristotle', and 'heirs to centuries of logical analysis',[3] should beware of a too literal understanding of the words. *Wind* (2) and *fire* (3) were an accepted symbolism for the powerful and cleansing operation of God's Spirit.[4] In this event God was manifesting Himself uniquely at a vital moment in history. The impact of God's Being upon men, of His other world on this, produced the

[1] *Leviticus* in the *Expositor's Bible* (Eerdmans' 1956 edition), 1, pp. 352 f.
[2] *The Acts of the Apostles (Moffatt Commentary)*, pp. 4, 9. Dr. Foakes-Jackson admits 'reserve' in the account of the ascension, but seems to contradict this admission a few lines lower by speaking of Luke's 'dramatic method of narration'.
[3] C. S. Lewis, *op. cit.*, p. 188.
[4] See Cruden's *Concordance* under both words.

phenomena which mortal sense apprehended under the figures of this narrative.

The nature of the *tongues* (4) is very difficult to determine. The following points must be taken into account. First, those men listed in verses 9 to 11 are mainly Jews resident among the peoples named. They are those of the Dispersion who were on religious pilgrimage to Jerusalem, and who would understand the two languages of Palestine, Aramaic and Greek. A few foreigners would be among their number, proselytes of the synagogues. These would certainly know Greek, and possibly Aramaic. No multiple gift of tongues was therefore necessary. But, secondly, if the gift was indeed of this nature, as a first reading of Luke's account seems to imply, and as most commentators have assumed, it was a gift which was rapidly withdrawn. Paul was trilingual by education. We see him speak with equal facility to the Sanhedrin and the Areopagus, and converse with representatives of the Roman army. In a district where neither Aramaic, nor Greek, nor Latin served him (xiv. 11–14), he and Barnabas failed to perceive the development of an embarrassing situation because its beginnings were obscured by an alien tongue. Thirdly, this was in spite of the fact that Paul had 'spoken with tongues' after the fashion discussed in 1 Cor. xii and xiv (and probably in Acts x. 46 and xix. 6). It is generally assumed that this phenomenon, which Paul endeavours to tone down, is a species of ecstatic utterance, tolerated as a passing phase and because the most devoted spirits in the Church were subject to it. Furthermore, to be useful in worship, this type of utterance required an interpreter. None was needed at Pentecost.

It would therefore appear that the phenomenon of Acts ii was not exactly that of Corinth, and later incidents in Acts. What then was it? It is impossible to be dogmatic, a fact which the diversity of opinion among competent and orthodox authorities will illustrate. R. B. Rackham,[1] for example, holds that Acts ii speaks of the glossolalia of Corinth, and that it was worship, not evangelism, which was the subject of the utter-

[1] *Op. cit.*, p. 21.

ance. Peter alone preached. Rackham admits that 'verses 8 and 11 require that some of the utterances should, as was natural, have been clothed in foreign words'. It is, of course, to be supposed that the ecstatic glossolaly would, in a polyglot world, contain such intrusions of alien vocabulary. F. F. Bruce[1] writes: 'The disciples, suddenly delivered from the peculiarities of their Galilean speech, praised God and rehearsed His mighty works in such a way that each hearer recognized with surprise his own native language or dialect. . . . The Corinthian glossolalia does not seem to have been quite the same as this. . . .' Bruce points out that all the hearers spoke Greek or Aramaic, and so seems to imply that the Pentecostal gift was purified and exalted utterance which removed dialectical barriers to understanding. In another context[2] he remarks that 'the disciples were heard praising God in languages and dialects diverse from their native Galilean Aramaic, but recognizable by visitors to the feast as those which some of them spoke.'

Among liberal commentators there is a similar hesitancy. F. J. Foakes-Jackson[3] is peculiarly difficult to follow. Consider, for example, the following three statements in juxtaposition. They are found on one page: 'Indeed, if the author of Acts were a companion of the Apostle, he must have known that the common phenomenon of "speaking with tongues" did not in any way resemble what is recorded to have taken place in Acts ii. . . .' 'In short, despite the fact that the Galilean language was considered to be corrupt in Jerusalem, Galilean believers could be widely understood, and the fact that every man heard them in his own tongue may be explained as allegorical of the future diffusion of the gospel to all nations . . .'; '. . . some sneered and derided those who had received the Spirit as drunken. . . . On the other hand, if the tongues were like those alluded to in 1 Corinthians, it was a perfectly natural criti-

---

[1] *The Acts of the Apostles*, p. 82.
[2] *The New Bible Commentary*, p. 902.
[3] *Op. cit.*, p. 12.

cism. . . .' A. W. F. Blunt,[1] with less than adequate respect for Luke's capacity as an historian, sees the Corinthian glossolalia in the Pentecostal phenomenon, but suggests that the facts have been 'amplified by tradition into a rhapsody', not without reference to a mystic reversal of Babel. (The latter significance would have been accepted on more orthodox grounds by the older commentators.[2])

To sum up: it seems reasonable, mainly on the grounds that such a miracle would serve no immediately practicable purpose, to reject the view that foreign languages were spoken by those who had no knowledge of them, and who, as far as our information goes, promptly forgot them. The lack of any need for 'interpreters' makes it difficult to identify the situation with that which Paul seeks to regulate in the Corinthian church. The 'tongues' made for clarity, they did not destroy it. On the other hand, it must be admitted that sympathy made for understanding. The scoffers merely heard the incoherencies of intoxication (13). This may, in fact, be a point for R. B. Rackham. This much is certain: the atmosphere was charged with the holiest excitement. In the moments of high emotion simple men, forgetting self and its limitations, sometimes speak with a penetrating clarity and a compelling precision beyond their commoner capabilities. What emancipation might come to tongue and mind under the conviction of a present manifestation of God Himself? Could it be that lips so prepared spoke that day to hearts prepared, with speech so pure, that sincere men felt an intimacy of understanding, a correspondence in what was uttered to the pattern of their deepest longings, in a way so beyond their experience that each could truly say that the speakers, or some one of them, spoke 'in his own tongue'? This much at least is true. If more is true, that wider margin must be a matter of individual opinion and of faith. A miracle undoubtedly was involved.

---

[1] *Acts* in the *Clarendon Bible*, p. 317.
[2] E.g. G. T. Stokes in the *Expositor's Bible* (Eerdmans' 1956 edition), v, p. 320.

Additional Notes

i. 1. The significance of the title bestowed on Theophilus in the earlier address (Lk. i. 3) may be gathered from later contexts in Acts (xxiii. 26, xxiv. 3, xxvi. 25). It seems to indicate equestrian rank. (Ramsay, *op. cit.*, pp. 65–71.)

i. 12. The *sabbath day's journey* is based on Ex. xvi. 29 and xxxi. 13; cf. Nu. xxxv. 5, 26, 27. Those interested in the nonsense with which the literalism of the Rabbis cluttered the application and interpretation of the Law will find a note in J. R. Lumby (*op. cit.*, p. 85).

ii. 5. The word used for *devout* (*eulabēs*) is one of those words which Christianity elevated. In Classical Greek it meant merely 'discreet' or 'cautious'. Luke uses it of good and godly men (e.g. Lk. ii. 25; Acts viii. 2), and it often appears in this higher sense in Christian inscriptions (e.g. C.I. 8615 and 8647).

ii. 8. Greek throws no light on the problem of this verse. The word translated *tongue* is *dialektos*, but the word in Greek has a wider significance than its derivation, and can mean 'language' as well as 'dialect'.

ii. 13. There was no *new wine* at Pentecost. August was the nearest vintage. The Greek means 'sweet wine', the product of a certain type of grape, perhaps in favour at the time, or especially high in alcoholic content.

ii. 15. Scrupulous Jews drank wine only with flesh, and, on the authority of Ex. xvi. 8, ate bread in the morning and flesh only in the evening. Hence wine could be drunk only in the evening. This is the point of Peter's remark.

II. THE CHURCH IN ACTION (ii. 14–iv. 31)

a. Peter's first sermon (ii. 14–40)

Peter's theme reveals the message of the first evangelists long before the New Testament was written, and provides a complete answer to the allegation that Pauline theology changed beyond recognition the simple teaching of Jesus Christ. This is not, of course, to maintain that the marks of an earlier evangelism are not discernible in the sermon. Some Pauline touches are absent, but, as F. F. Bruce remarks, 'that this should be so in a report written by a Gentile, and by one who came so much under Paul's influence as Luke did, is a compelling token of the genuineness of these speeches.'[1] Peter very naturally speaks to a Jewish audience (see comment above, p. 55, concerning the constitution of the crowd) in terms of Messianic expectation.

Two further points should be stressed. First, the reference based on Joel to the outpouring of the Spirit *upon all flesh* (17), and the extension of this phrase in verse 39, does not imply that Peter already envisaged the truths he was compelled to learn in the events and experiences described in chapters x and xv. Sir George Adam Smith[2] justly insists that Peter meant no more than Joel meant. Those *that are afar off* (39) would naturally be supposed to approach Christianity by way of Judaism. Nor, secondly, is the command to *be baptized* (38) a fussy copyist's insertion of a later practice. Peter was familiar enough with Christian baptism (Jn. iv. 1, 2), and saw in it an act of witness, as well as Jewry's familiar ritual of purification. Paul's writings were to enrich the doctrine of baptism, but it was natural enough that Peter should continue a practice of Jesus and John.

Peter appropriately began by firmly anchoring his theme in Scripture familiar to his audience (14, 22). Without limitation of age (17), or of condition (18), God was to claim servants for His Word, as Christ Himself had already claimed them, by the sea, under the fig-tree, at the receipt of custom. His chosen were to *prophesy* (18), that is, to interpret spiritual truth. Jerusalem, in fact, was seeing this happen. Verses 19 and 20 telescope, as Old Testament prophecy frequently does, the coming of Christ, the day of His grace, and future judgment.

[1] *Op. cit.*, p. 96.
[2] *Joel* in the *Expositor's Bible* (Eerdmans' 1956 edition), IV, p. 664.

Seeing before him the very crowd of the Passion Week, those whose voices had cried 'Hosanna . . . Barabbas . . . Crucify', Peter turns sternly to the central truth of the gospel. The cross was part of God's plan (23), but the guilt was still theirs who delivered Christ to its agony and shame. Such evil was frustrated, for God raised Christ from the dead. This claim, be it noted, was not advanced in some far corner of the world, but in Jerusalem, where the fact of the empty tomb, whatever hostility made of it, must have been common knowledge.

Furthermore, that triumph was rooted in familiar Scripture. Peter quotes Ps. xvi. 8–11, a passage also quoted by Paul (xiii. 35). The psalm is an utterance of David's days of exile. 'Men and brethren,' pleads the preacher, turning from sternness to pity as the subject grips him, 'consider what David must have meant, he whose white tomb is visible before you. In the grip of inspiration he spoke of events beyond his ken, and you are witnesses of the fulfilment.' In his First Epistle (i. 10–12) Peter further expounds this view of Old Testament prophecy.

Catching an echo from well-remembered words (Mt. xxii. 41–46), Peter passes to Ps. cx. 1. It was Paul's theme of Phil. ii. 9–11, expressed in Peter's allusive manner. Jesus, crucified and risen, has also been exalted. Verse 36 returns to the fearless thrust of verse 23, and the final appeal is by way of a postscript, the answer to a question of convicted men (37–40). Note the clarity with which the issues are made evident (38). Repentance demands the witness of baptism; forgiveness is followed by the gift of the Holy Spirit.

Verse 39 reveals Peter himself as a prophet speaking words pregnant with a larger meaning after the fashion of the Old Testament prophets, as he himself understood them. Peter still saw before him a purified and emancipated Judaism, but his words suggest a vision and a passion which opened the way to later illumination.

Note finally verse 40. Luke is reporting in brief outline, and the marks of Peter's own manner are so notable in this abstract of his sermon, that it seems likely that an Aramaic record was kept among the documents of the Church. It is too readily forgotten that the age was literate.

b. First rapture (ii. 41-47)

This section is a most important historical passage picturing the Church in its primitive form. F. J. Foakes-Jackson,[1] while admitting that the number of *three thousand* converts (41) is 'not as incredible as some are disposed to think', states that the description here briefly given 'is ideal rather than historical'. Apart from mentioning Luke's well-founded claim to veracity, it may be pointed out that chapters v and vi speak with great frankness of very human faults in the Church. As for the number of the converts, it must be remembered that the ministry of the Son of God had recently ended in Jerusalem amid events of shattering emotional power, that the disappearance of His body was incontrovertible fact, and had found a place in preaching, and that Pentecost itself was an experience hardly to be contained. Add the fact that the audience, at a time of high religious festival, was composed of those who, in numberless cases, were instructed Jews and proselytes, prepared in heart for the movement and revelation of God.

In this picture of the early Church note, first, the mode of entrance (41). This was no loose group, but a clear-cut society, universal in membership, but with definite, firm standards. Repentance, confession, and baptism were necessary. Secondly, the authority of the apostles (Mt. xxviii. 18-20) is recognized from the first (42). Thirdly, fellowship is the keynote. The 'lovefeast' (*breaking of bread*, 42) includes the Lord's Supper, but was later separated from it. Eating together, especially in the East, has always been a prime sign of fellowship. There is perhaps room for the revival of 'the common meal'. Fourthly, the experiment in a kind of communism of goods (45) did not spread. Imperfect tenses are used: 'they used to sell . . . used to divide. . . .' Lastly, joy and the respect of the multitude (46 f.), and continual effectiveness ('the Lord was adding

[1] *Op. cit.*, pp. 18, 21.

daily . . . those who were being saved') were the natural fruits
of such united testimony.

c. At the Beautiful Gate (iii. *1–11*)

Commentators, who have failed to appreciate the pattern of
Luke's historiography, have imagined chapter iii to contain
some duplication of chapter ii. The theory hardly needs
refutation, but note in passing two points of sequence between
this section and the last. Luke has mentioned 'wonders and
signs' (ii. 43); here is one of them, singled out because it led
directly to the Sadducean persecution. The continued loyalty
of the converted Jews to the temple services was mentioned in
ii. 46; here, then, are Peter and John proceeding thither, and
finding occasion for action and word *in the name of Jesus* (6).

R. J. Knowling,[1] remarking on the vividness of the narrative,
suggests that the details came from Peter himself. Such vividness is characteristic of Mark's Gospel, of which Peter is
regarded as the chief source. The same phenomenon, whether
the style is Mark's own or Peter's, is to be seen in chapter xii,
another Marcan-Petrine context. It has also been noticed that
terms found frequently in the medical writers are prominent
in verse 7. In fact, the passage is an interesting study in
reporting.

The more myopic of the commentators (for example Zeller
and Overbeck), mightily conscious of the trees and unable to
appreciate the wood, have marked the fact that there is no
prominence given to the cripple's faith. Luke, as the authority
responsible for the story, is supposed thus to magnify the magic
of the miracle. It has often been the fate of Scripture to be
treated with a scepticism which no-one would apply to documents of secular history. Set within the context of New
Testament healing, the story quite obviously implies that the
man was healed by faith. Faith was seen and blessed in the
brief interchange of look and word by which Peter disclaimed
the possibility of alms, but offered something more precious
(4–7). Like Paul (xiv. 9) at Lystra, Peter saw that the man 'had

[1] *Op. cit.*, II, p. 107.

faith to be healed'. Verse 6, in fact, is a test of faith, for the words *Jesus of Nazareth* had recently appeared above a 'malefactor's' cross. Note, too, the man's immediate association of himself with his benefactors, and his frank and open gratitude to God.

d. Peter's second sermon (iii. 12-26)

It is difficult to see how anyone could set aside this muscular and powerful address as a confused duplicate of the Pentecostal message. It falls into two parts. First, Peter begins with a fearless proclamation of the Lord's Messiahship. This is obscured in the AV, which renders *pais* as *Son* and *child* (13; see also iii. 26, iv. 27, 30). It should be translated 'Servant' (RV), and clearly recalls the most solemn of the Old Testament prophecies, the 'Servant passages' of the later chapters of Isaiah. Peter's word could be trusted to set Jewish minds moving through those familiar and challenging oracles. This was the Being they had done to death, and in charging them thus Peter echoes the contrasts woven into the Isaian prophecies. God glorified His Servant; the Jews betrayed Him (13). Pilate acquitted Him; the Jews denied Him (13). He was the Holy One and the Just; the Jews chose a murderer (14). The Jews killed Him; God raised Him from the dead (15).

Secondly, after the manner of his first sermon, Peter turns, at verse 17, from stern denunciation to appeal. Let them repent, for their vast evil has not frustrated God. Christ's passion was in God's purpose. Verse 18 should be translated 'his Christ' (RV), that is, 'His Anointed'. It is a quotation from Ps. ii. 2, which Peter uses again in fuller form in iv. 26. Christ is still the living and the coming Saviour, as the resurrection shows (19-21). Peter's main concern is to remove the Jews' stumbling-block, the offence of the cross. The first and most necessary step in this Jewish evangel was to prove from the testimony of the prophets that the sufferings of the Messiah were part of God's plan. The argument from verses 19 to 25 may sound to western ears a trifle remote, but it would be illuminating and cogent to minds trained in the thought-forms and language of the Old Testament. Notice the lofty Christ-ology: 'Jesus Christ of Nazareth' of verse 6 is 'the Holy and Righteous One' (14), 'the Prince of life' (15), 'God's Christ' (18), 'God's Servant' (13, 26). The great doctrines later developed in the writings of Paul and John are all latent here. It is objected by F. J. Foakes-Jackson[1] that 'there are many words in this speech which it is hard to believe that a Galilean peasant could have used'. It is relevant to point out that the peasant concerned had spent three years in the presence of Jesus Christ, that before that experience he had been under the influence and teaching of one whom Christ described as the greatest of the prophets, and that he came fresh from the Pentecostal coming of the Holy Spirit, with every memory of past instruction, every detail of experience, every native faculty, stirred and fired by the divine Visitant. Add finally the fact that, however else one may choose to describe him, Peter was a notable figure of ancient history.

e. The Sadducean persecution (iv. 1-7)

The Sadducees held by tradition the high-priestly office. Collaborators with the Roman order, rationalists in doctrine, they were sensitive of everything likely to disturb the comfortable status they had won (cf. Jn. xi. 47-50), and especially saw danger in popular excitement arising from such Pharisaic teaching as that of the resurrection. (Note the lead they assumed over the Pharisees in persecuting Christ, when the question of Lazarus arose (Jn. xii. 10).)

They now see a familiar pattern of events: a notable miracle (cf. iv. 16 and Jn. xi. 47); the preaching of the resurrection, and that in the case of One whom they had put to death; a challenge to prestige (2). (The Christian's right to teach has stirred the jealousy of hierarchies throughout history.) In the Greek text of verse 7 there is scornful emphasis on *ye*, which comes last in the sentence.

[1] *Op. cit.*, p. 29.

f. Peter's third sermon (iv. 8–12)

It is impossible to state to what extent Peter's defence has been abbreviated. As it stands in the text it is a gem of concentrated evangelism, and contains, for all its brevity, the familiar features of his style. Notice that the audience is addressed with all respect; the hearers' own experience is referred to; facts are proclaimed fearlessly; the appeal is clear and uncompromising; Scripture is aptly quoted, and just how aptly the recollection of Mt. xxi. 42 (=Mk. xii. 10; Lk. xx. 17) will indicate. *The stone which was set at nought* (11) is an Old Testament symbol (Ps. cxviii. 22; Is. xxviii. 16) which was taken up in the New Testament and referred to Jesus Christ (e.g. 1 Pet. ii. 7), rejected of men but destined to be the chief corner-stone of the temple in which all nations are one (1 Cor. iii. 11; Eph. ii. 20). Such was Luke's literary art that he compressed into ninety words of Greek the point, power, and purport of this brave and aggressive defence.

g. Conflict (iv. 13–31)

Sir William Ramsay[1] draws attention to verses 13–18 as typical of Luke's historical style. 'The Jewish leaders perceived the bold and fluent speech of Peter and John; and yet they observed from their dress and style of utterance that they were not trained scholars . . . and they further took notice of the fact that they were the disciples of Jesus; and they gazed on the man that had been cured standing along with his preservers. These were the facts of the case. . . . The historian's point is that there is only one possible inference; and as the Jewish leaders were unwilling to draw that inference, they perforce kept silence not having the wherewithal to dispute the obvious conclusion . . . that these illiterate fishermen had acquired the art and power of effective oratory through their having been the disciples of Jesus, and through the divine grace and power communicated to them.' That is forcefully said, though a question-mark might be put against Ramsay's use of the word 'illiterate'.

[1] *St. Paul the Traveller and Roman Citizen*, p. 371.

Note the following points. First, John also spoke (13). Luke assumes that his readers will be acquainted with procedure and quotes the more effective utterance. Secondly, the character of the Lord is contagious. Compare verses 13 and 14 with Jn. vii. 46. Thirdly, the persecutors' typical desire to silence truth (17, 18). Fourthly, in a stylist like Luke, it is important to watch every word; for example, the man was *standing* among them (14).

Having clashed thus with authority, the apostles, in these days of acute awareness and insight, were conscious that they were laying down principles for the Church. Their action, in fact, was to guide the Church through three (or is it nineteen?) centuries of persecution. A decision to defy authority was not lightly taken, and the occasion called for guidance. Hence the prayer found in verses 24 to 30. It is not a primitive hymn of the Church, as it has sometimes been called, but a prayer of Peter, saturated with the terminology of Scripture, in which the assembly joined *with one accord* (24). Note the marks of a now familiar voice: the appeal to Scripture (25, 26); the preoccupation with the cross (27, 28); a valiant humility (29, 30). Like Hezekiah (Is. xxxvii. 14), Peter spread his trouble before the Lord, laid down no presumptuous procedure, called for no vengeance, and left God to act. God did (31).

Additional Notes

ii. 23. An examination of the language and doctrinal emphasis of the First Epistle of Peter reinforces the impression that Luke's report is based on a script. For example the word *foreknowledge* occurs again at 1 Pet. i. 2, and nowhere else in the New Testament.

ii. 25. Translate 'saw', not *foresaw*. The AV is translating a word of the Common Dialect as if it were Classical Greek.

ii. 27. 'Hades' (RV) not *hell*. In meaning, and probably in derivation, the word means 'the unseen world'.

ii. 41. It is not impossible that *day* means 'a period of time', and that the text should not be pressed to mean that twenty-four hours saw the conviction, conversion, and baptism of three thousand. The issues were rooted in one day, or one compact period referred to as a day saw the process complete.

ii. 47. Manuscript evidence is against the inclusion of the phrase *to the church*. The meaning is independent of the phrase. The final phrase *such as should be saved* awkwardly renders a present participle, 'those being saved'.

iii. 13. 'When he had determined' (RV), not *when he was determined*. There was decision, not mere purpose involved.

iv. 7. *By what power*: the prosecutors use *dunamis*, not *exousia*, which contains the notion of authority. The implication is that the apostles had acted by illegal incantation and the processes of magic.

iv. 17. *Straitly threaten* is a rendering of a Hebraism which has found its way into the Greek text, a not uncommon phenomenon as may be seen in J. H. Moulton's paragraph on the subject (*Grammar of New Testament Greek*, ii, pp. 443 f.). It occurs again, similarly rendered, at v. 28. The interest attaching to both contexts is the flavour of original reporting. Was Paul present, and did he remember the idiom of the priests, and report it to Luke in a somewhat literal translation?

iv. 28. The word translated *determined* is used by only Luke and Paul, but is in striking conformity with Peter's thought (ii. 23, x. 42; 1 Pet. i. 2, 20, ii. 4–6). A study of Peter's thought and vocabulary in utterances reported in Acts and in his own writing demonstrates most convincingly their unity.

iv. 30. The 'medical language' of Luke has not been marked in detail in these notes. F. F. Bruce lists the authorities (*The Acts of the Apostles*, pp. 4 f.). The temptation in all such specialized word-studies is to collect evidence too uncritically. In iv. 30, however, it may be noted that the word translated *to heal* is a noun (*iasis*) used elsewhere twice by Luke and nowhere else in the New Testament. The corresponding verb is used twice as many times by Luke as by the other three evangelists together. Both terms are good medical vocabulary. The subject may rest there with the final remark that Luke's Greek is strong evidence for the authenticity of Acts.

III. 'MID TOIL AND TRIBULATION (iv. 32–v. 42)

a. The Church in unity (iv. 32–37)

R. J. Knowling[1] deals conclusively with the notion that this passage is a 'doublet' of ii. 44, 45. 'The same spirit prevails in both accounts,' he writes, 'but in the one case we have the immediate result of the Pentecostal gift, in the case before us we have the permanence, and not only the vitality of the gift marked—the Christian community is now organised under Apostolic direction, and stress is laid upon the continuance of the "first love", whilst the contrast is marked between the self-sacrifice of Barnabas, and the greed of Ananias and Sapphira.'

The historian's purpose, in short, is as follows. He is writing episodically, and considers the story of Ananias and Sapphira important. It was necessary to preface that story with further reference to the experiment in 'communism'. It is also, more remotely, introductory to the institution of the diaconate in chapter vi. It was, further, necessary to indicate a time-lapse between the incidents of the first Sadducean persecution and the domestic tragedy of the Church. These verses suggest a period of single-minded activity and consolidation between the well-remembered prayer-meeting (iv. 23–31) and the sad events of chapter v. Finally, occasion is simultaneously taken to introduce, in Luke's manner (cf. vi. 5, vii. 58), a future protagonist of the Church, and one whose example stands in contrast to the conduct of Ananias and Sapphira.

As regards details, note that the community of goods was not compulsory (v. 4). Secondly, the final phrase of iv. 34 perhaps indicates that varying portions were sold according

[1] *Op. cit.*, II, p. 138.

to the conscience of individuals. Thirdly, Barnabas is picked out as a notable example of one who sold his possessions, made the money over, and lived by the work of his hands. Fourthly, an immature view of the second advent was responsible for some of this enthusiasm. The situation in Jerusalem was later paralleled in Thessalonica, as Paul's Epistles to that church show. In Thessalonica an unnatural excitement led to abandonment of work; in Jerusalem it prompted a reckless generosity which nevertheless did credit to the love and devotion of those concerned. Fifthly, the poverty of the Jerusalem church, which later called for world-wide charity, may have been occasioned by this over-hasty dissipation of capital. Lastly, a mitigating circumstance, when the subject is viewed from the vantage-point of history, is the fact that most of the property thus turned into cash and then used, no doubt perished in the catastrophes of AD 67–70.

b. The Church divided (v. 1–11)

This story should not be approached emotionally. Peter was severe, and the fate of the two delinquents shocking, but the strictures of Christ on hypocrisy must be borne in mind (Mt. xxiii). It must have been intensely painful for Luke, after writing four chapters of triumphant history, to turn now to record a tale of sordid ·deception. He was not, however, writing biased propaganda, but the truth. It has been pointed out above that the contributions described were sacrificial, not compulsory. The old 'leaven of the Pharisees' was at work, and for the first time in the community of the saints two persons set out deliberately to deceive their leaders and their friends, to build a reputation for sanctity and sacrifice to which they had no right, and to menace, in so doing, all love, all trust, all sincerity. And not only was the sin against human brotherhood, but against the Spirit of God, so recently and powerfully manifest in the Church. It required some hardihood of wickedness to lie and pose in such an atmosphere. 'So familiar are we with "spots and wrinkles" in the Church', writes Rackham,[1]

[1] *Op. cit.*, p. 64.

'that we can with difficulty realize the significance of this, the first sin in and against the community. . . . It corresponds to the entrance of the serpent into Eden . . . and the first fall from the ideal must have staggered the apostles and the multitude.'

Rackham[1] notes something 'Hebraic' about the narrative, and that is a fact which an ear attuned to the Old Testament will recognize. The story is told with reserve, and there is no evidence of those extravagances and accretions which are the invariable mark of legend. At the same time those details which might interest an antiquarian, but which do nothing to advance the purpose of the book, are omitted. For example, although we are uninformed on the matter, it is probable that there were certain formalities connected with a sudden death, both social and civil, which required fulfilment, but which find no mention here. Interest is confined to what Rackham calls 'the prophetic elements' in the story.

c. The second persecution (v. 12-26)

The shock to the Church was also a challenge. Luke gives us another brief account of its unity and activity. Verses 13 and 14 require elucidation. It was common enough practice in both Athens and Jerusalem for like-minded groups to gather for instruction and discussion in the courts or porticos of public buildings. The Christians met habitually in Solomon's porch (12), and enjoyed such a reputation with the people at large that no one lightly frequented their gatherings (13). It will be seen, when Paul's speech before the Areopagus is discussed, that a 'corona', or ring of bystanders, may have been within hearing of the court. There is a consciousness of such an audience discernible in more than one context of ancient oratory. Nor was the situation dissimilar in Jerusalem; for example, the bystanders in the high priest's courtyard were clearly within sound of the proceedings in the assembly-hall in the high priest's house (Jn. xviii). In the case of the Christian gathering in Solomon's porch, people generally felt a respect

[1] *Op. cit.*, p. 67.

which inhibited the common curiosity of the place and time, and which led to many conversions (14). Verses 15 and 16 describe a time of considerable excitement, and the situation must again be viewed within its context of place and time. Even in more reserved communities a religious revival is apt to be accompanied by a certain emotional tension, and even leads to superstitious practice (15), but this is not to deny or to minimize the spiritual genuineness of such movements.

The Sanhedrin, at any rate, saw their worst fears realized. They viewed with alarm anything in the nature of popular tumult, and indeed, in such an inflammable province, a high level of excitement in the populace opened the way danger-ously for the rabble-rousing which fanatics sought to use, and which imperilled the unstable position of collaborating Jews. Arrest followed (18).

The second imprisonment called forth a divine intervention, and raises the perennial problem of miracles. One of the in-grained convictions of the modern mind is that law in the natural world, or what from the observance of a number of instances and examples it takes to be law, is not broken. In consequence a disturbance of the natural is looked upon as impossible, and an account of such a disturbance as mistaken or mendacious reporting. Such scepticism has its place and purpose in the history of thought, and no believer is called to credulity. At the same time it should be pointed out that the first act of faith is to believe in God, and God is sovereign over the works of His hands. The events of Luke's story are also those surrounding the greatest movement of God in human history after the ministry, death, and resurrection of Christ; the establishment, to wit, of His Church. Nor are the miracles of Scripture without significance. We note the renewed vigour of the apostles' evangelism, and their firm testimony. There must have been tonic, too, in God's revealed favour after the tragedy of Ananias.

Finally, note a remark of Ramsay,[1] who, beginning with profound scepticism, found himself, after a lifetime of study, a

[1] *St. Paul the Traveller and Roman Citizen*, p. 384.

most ardent champion of Luke. Luke, he states, 'everywhere follows with minute care the best authority accessible to him'. In this instance his authorities stood, at the time of the events described, on opposing sides, being no less than Peter and Paul.

d. In the Sanhedrin (v. 27–42)

The anger of the Sadducees had a double foundation. As the high priests they were blamed for the murder of Christ, and found a volatile Jerusalem beginning to grow hostile (28); they were also bitterly opposed to the teaching of resurrection, and here the hated doctrine was associated with the prophet whom they had found it expedient to remove (Jn. xi. 50).

Peter's defence is brief and clear. He sets forth an eternal principle (29), and relates the gospel to the traditional faith (30). He states facts regardless of his audience (30, 31), and he underlines the meaning of those facts (31). Finally he closes with a word of personal testimony. This fourth sermon of Peter is in the familiar style of his earlier pronouncements, even to habits of vocabulary, visible in spite of, or perhaps because of, the brevity and concision of the summary. It is, furthermore, a striking example of the promised enabling (Lk. xii. 11, 12).

Associated with the Sadducees were Pharisees who had shared the guilt of the death of Christ. One of the ablest of the Pharisees now states his policy. It is impossible to judge Gamaliel's motives exactly. They may have been political: Acts xxiii reveals the sharp division between the two parties in the Sanhedrin; or they may have been religious. The case against Peter differed from that soon to be levelled against Stephen. The apostles were regarded as pious Israelites, and no breach of temple or of legal tradition was alleged against them. As a wise follower of tradition, Gamaliel may therefore have seen no real cause for action. This line is quite consistent with what little is known of the speaker. The speech carried the day, and those who were 'sawn through' (so, literally, *cut to the heart*, 33) by Peter's fighting defence were driven to milder counsels. For disobedience the prisoners received the

Jewish penalty of 'forty stripes save one' (40) and were dismissed with a stern warning, which in no way influenced their Christian activity (42). It was an historic moment. For the first time Christians suffered in their bodies for their faith and honest preaching. So began in Peter's personal experience that which he put powerfully into his teaching (1 Pet. ii. 20, 21, iii. 14, 17, iv. 1, 12–19).

Additional Notes

iv. 37. A singular noun is used for *money* (*chrēma*). The plural is almost invariably used in this sense. Perhaps Lumby is right (*op. cit.*, p. 133) in suggesting that the singular is thus employed 'to indicate the compactness, the entirety of what was brought ... the sum without deduction, in contrast to the proceeding which follows in the next chapter'.

v. 8. *For so much* is probably deictic. Like Judas' thirty pieces, the sum lay on the floor, rejected and unclean.

v. 11. The *church* (*ekklēsia*) first finds mention here. The word, in the vocabulary of Greek democracy, meant the popular assembly gathered under its executive officers for the debate and discussion of the State's business. F. F. Bruce has a useful note, and references to authorities (*op. cit.*, p. 136).

v. 30. Translate 'whom you hanged on a tree and slew'. The aorist participle shows that the hanging 'on the tree' was anterior to the slaying, which seems to contravene the law in Dt. xxi. 22. The phrase is again used by Peter in x. 39, but appears nowhere else in the New Testament. It is also Peter who repeats the use of the word 'tree' for the instrument of crucifixion (1 Pet. ii. 24). The word (*xulon*) commonly means timber, 'wood' (1 Cor. iii. 12; Rev. xviii. 12), then, by synecdoche, a club, 'staves' (Mt. xxvi. 47, 55) and 'stocks' (Acts xvi. 24). This may be the origin of the use for a 'cross' which Peter twice employs and Paul once (v. 30, x. 39, xiii. 29). It is more likely that the AV translation reflects the true origin. In Hellenistic Greek the word was used sometimes for a living tree (Lk. xxiii. 31; Rev. ii. 7). The common word for the cross of crucifixion was *stauros*, or stake, and refers only to the up-right post on which the cross-beam carried by the victim (Jn. xix. 17) was fixed. This was a fixture at the place of execution and sawn-off tree-trunks no doubt provided a firmer post. The final shape was a T, not the familiar crucifix. The victim's hands were nailed (through the wrist) before the cross-beam was placed on the stake. For the whole shocking process, including an authoritative diagnosis of the cause of death, see the moving work by Dr. Pierre Barbet, *The Passion of our Lord Jesus Christ*. The French surgeon is preoccupied with the authenticity of the Turin Shroud, but his amazing investigation of the horrors of crucifixion is independent of this theme.

IV. THE HELLENISTIC JEWS (vi. 1–viii. 40)

a. The deacons (vi. 1–7)

The purpose of this section, like that of iv. 32–37, is twofold. It is quite in Luke's manner. It describes an important advance in organization, and points to the rift in outlook between the Hellenistic and Hebrew sections of the Church. Out of this situation rose Stephen, a vital link in the story as it moves on to the ministry of Paul. The passage might be regarded as an epilogue to the story so far told, or a preface to the third persecution and the conversion of Paul.

The members of the Christian community are called *disciples* (1), the term appropriate in the Gospels for those who gathered round the divine Teacher, but destined to give place to the 'brethren' and the 'saints' of the Epistles. In the synoptists 'disciple' occurs one hundred and sixty times, in John seventy-eight times, in Acts twenty-eight times, and in the rest of the New Testament not at all. 'During the lifetime of Jesus', writes W. Sanday,[1] 'the disciples were called after their relation to Him; after His departure the names given to them indicated their relation to each other and to the society.'

A second case of difficulty within the Church has appeared,

[1] *Inspiration*, p. 289.

but is dealt with effectively, promptly, and generously. Note the leadership of the Twelve in a thoroughly democratic fellowship (2, 3), and the recognition that an expanding society demanded organization. The Seven are never actually called 'deacons', and may be regarded as special officers appointed to meet a special need. They also undertook spiritual work (8). From their names it appears that those chosen were themselves Greek Jews. If so, the choice reveals the graciousness of the Church.

b. Stephen's ministry (vi. 8–15)

Notable among the Hellenistic Jews was Stephen, who soon became known for a new and startling interpretation of the gospel. Since he stands in the direct spiritual ancestry of Paul, his teaching and ministry must be carefully noted. His teaching first drove a wedge between Judaism and Christianity, and ensured the distinctiveness of the Christian Church. The first five chapters of Acts show large numbers of Jews accepting the new faith, but it is unlikely that they saw in the act a repudiation of Judaism. 'Stephen', writes A. W. F. Blunt,[1] 'seems to have brought over with him into Christianity ideas and a point of view which he may have learnt from the more liberal Judaism of the Dispersion.' Neither nationalism nor conservatism were unknown in the communities of dispersed Jewry. Paul's own father was a Pharisee, and he himself encountered bigotry in overseas synagogues. On the whole, however, there was a tendency among the Jews of the Dispersion to subordinate the ceremonial to the moral law, and to allow latitude to Gentile converts.

Stephen's ministry notably foreshadowed Paul's in his spiritual interpretation of the Law. Orthodox Jewry was quick to see that his teaching involved the supersession of Judaism, or its sublimation into Christianity (see verses 13, 14). 'It is true', says Blunt in the note already quoted, 'that he emphasizes the spirit of the Law rather than the letter, while Paul tends rather to recoil altogether from the Law, as from some-

[1] *Op. cit.*, p. 160.

thing which by the rigidity of its letter sterilizes any spirit that was in it. . . . But Stephen's ideas are such as reappear in Paul, with the difference due to the intensity of Paul's personal experience of the Law; and by his teaching Stephen broke the ground for Paul's universalism.'

c. Stephen's speech (vii. 1–53)

Alone of ancient peoples, the Jew saw in history the out-working of a divine plan and divine law. Repeatedly we see the faithful of the Old Testament turn to the past to trace again a story of mercy and deliverance. Stephen stands on familiar ground when he returns to *Abraham* (2–8), and shows how not only Moses but all history, when set in clear perspective, culminated in Jesus of Nazareth. In other words, he took the tradition his accusers professed to defend, and turned it with eloquence and deadly logic against its self-styled champions.

Joseph (9–16) and *Moses* (20–43), he suggests with subtle irony, were 'types', forecasting the treatment which Stephen's hearers had meted out to Jesus Christ. Joseph's brethren, rejecting the beloved of their father, Moses' people, turning with scorn and cursing on the one who only sought to give them freedom—these were prototypes which the audience would not fail to refer to themselves. The stories, it should be realized by the modern reader, were familiar enough. It was the angle which was new, the telling slant with its pointing finger of accusation. Verse 25 is a particularly clear example of this oratory.

Stephen naturally lingers over Moses, 'in whom they trusted' (Jn. v. 45–47), showing that the lawgiver, rejected by his people (35), foreshadowed the experience of Christ (Jn. i. 11). He also received the promise of the Messiah (37). It followed that preaching Christ was not disloyalty to an ancient tradition, but its fulfilment. This was powerful argument, and a continuation of Peter's theme (iii. 22, 23). (This truth was to be more fully developed for similar minds in the Epistle to the Hebrews; see iii. 1–6, ix. 18–20, xii. 24.) In

Jn. vi. 30–32 it is recorded that a miracle of Christ, witnessed by their own eyes, was discounted by the prejudiced audience, who compared it unfavourably with a miracle of Moses' day. Hence the necessity here for close and vigorous argument, as Stephen maintains that he exalts Moses by linking him with Christ. Note a verbal echo which might have been powerful in the spoken defence. '*This* Jesus of Nazareth', they had said in the accusation (vi. 14). '*This* Moses', echoes Stephen (35, 37, 38, 40) quoting their own forefathers' pronoun used in the moment when they rejected him (Ex. xxxii. 1). The story of the rejection of Moses then becomes very pointed and personal. Israel had scorned her deliverer (40), and the rebels worshipped their own handiwork. So in a sense were they doing again. The rebels fell under the judgment of blindness (42). So it was with Stephen's accusers.

In vi. 13, 14 the temple is mentioned before Moses. Stephen there reversed the order in the interests of logic. In vii. 47, having dealt with Moses, he passes to the temple. Throughout his speech he has, of course, been undermining the superstition which exalted a place of worship. The first great revelations of God had, in fact, taken place in foreign lands, Ur, Sinai, Midian, long before the temple existed (2–4, 29–34, 44–50). There were patriarchs actually buried in despised Samaria. The noble truth of verse 49 crowns this argument. Indeed it was the *tabernacle* which was expressly ordered of God (44). That lovely tent, with its empty holy place, where the cherubim gazed on the unoccupied seat above the tablets of the Law and the sprinkled blood, had been God's answer to the rebellion of Exodus xxxii, and was exquisite symbolism of all Stephen was preaching. God was with His people, sharing sun, wind, and suffering, beautiful but invisible, and to be approached only by way of sacrifice and the Law. The temple, Stephen implies, was a royal whim, tolerated of God. Such was the story of the Jews and their leaders, and resistance to God, persecution of the prophets, and violation of the real spirit of the Law, ran like a muddy trail from end to end of it (51–53). The Hellenistic Jew has spoken. No holy land, no exalted temple, gave men without spiritual insight a right to higher claim of privilege. Such a spirit had been that in which Joseph, Moses, the prophets, had been rejected, even as they had but recently rejected *the Just One* (52). The Law was holy, but had been spurned by murderers.

d. Stephen's martyrdom (vii. 54–viii. 4)

Nothing was more calculated to stir the ire of orthodox Jewry. Stephen had turned the witness of Moses against them. With consummate skill, in a speech which Paul clearly echoed in Pisidian Antioch (see Acts xiii. 14–41), he turned the whole history of the Jewish race into account, showing that its persecutions still ran true to form, and that all in which they falsely trusted had meaning and fulfilment only in Christ.

The scene in the Sanhedrin was tense, and Luke probably writes from Paul's own description. It reads like the story of the trial of Christ. Rackham[1] remarks: 'Like Jesus, Stephen was accused of blasphemy, and by false witnesses; even the charge ran in almost the same words, "destroy the temple". To both, the high priest made appeal: but there the parallel ends. Christ held His peace: the disciple made a speech of defence.'

The persecutor through the ages has sought to quench ideas by destroying the person who holds them, to frustrate the spirit by crushing the flesh. The trial was held, no doubt, in the temple-court, and was skilfully transformed into a riot. The Gospels are evidence enough that the Jewish leaders had the measure of Pilate. On this occasion their outbreak either surprised him, or intimidated him. Pilate's patron, Seianus, had fallen. He himself was recalled about AD 36, and during the closing years of his governorship must have considered his position painfully insecure. He probably judged it wise not to interfere with this Jewish brain-storm.

Stephen was dragged out of the sacred precinct, and those who stoned him *laid down their clothes at a young man's feet, whose*

[1] *Op. cit.*, p. 92.

name was Saul (58), a fact Paul later confesses with deep shame (xxii. 20). It was a turning-point in Paul's life.

The murder of Stephen precipitated a persecution which must have fallen most heavily on the Hellenistic Jews. Tolerated or in hiding, the apostles seem to have remained in Jerusalem. Pharisees and Sadducees were to some extent united, and the 'young man' Saul was the guiding spirit of evil. The account sets this time of tribulation in encouraging perspective. The forcible dispersion of the Jerusalem church was a rich source of evangelization. The chapter will show its influence reaching distant Ethiopia. It is noteworthy that, from this point onwards, the story proceeds in widening circles. It is also about to be revealed that the rabid persecutor was a tormented man, soon to be brought to surrender, and destined to be the greatest name in the history of the Church. So seldom is it possible to judge the true significance of events at the time of their occurrence.

e. Philip's ministry (viii. 5–40)

A section devoted to the brisk and refreshing ministry of Philip rounds off the interlude on the work of the Hellenistic Jews. Viewed as history, it provides Luke with a significant transition from the ministry of Peter to that of Paul. He is like Stephen in doctrine and outlook, like Paul in his evangelism, a clearly marked character with something of the Old Testament prophet about him.[1] Note the freshness of his methods. He moved here and there under the influence of the Spirit. His boldness, too, is notable. Following Christ's example (John iv), he took the gospel to the Samaritans (5).

It was in Samaria that the strange and sinister figure of *Simon* arose (9). Luke lays some emphasis on his story. Philip appears to have accepted this man's discipleship, and indeed his professed adherence to the Church may have been set down as a remarkable conversion. Verses 9 and 10 suggest that Simon was a charlatan, who professed to be some form of mediator with God. It has always been difficult for some minds to

[1] Rackham, *op. cit.*, p. 112.

realize that God is not remote, but ever ready to meet the questing and surrendered soul, open to the approach of faith, and not to be bought or persuaded by formulae or ritual. And all through the ages there have been those who have used this human quirk to usurp power. To persuade men that he possesses the secret of God's will, and the means of binding and conveying God's favour, has been the stock-in-trade of the imposter at all times. Simon was one such. He called himself *the great power of God* (10), and found the prestige which he had thus won a matter of some profit (11). Whether there was any measure of sincerity in his professed conversion it is impossible to say, but at this point Peter and John arrived to inspect the results of Philip's ministry.

They found much to commend, and it is to be noted that they received the Samaritan converts, and ministered to them (17). Peter was being prepared for a later and similar tour of inspection in a preaching circuit of Philip, and for a divine revelation he was to experience there (chapter x). But with Simon, Peter clashed, and with that forthrightness which has been his mark in Luke's narrative, he denounced the Samaritan wonder-worker as an imposter.

Concerning Simon the following should be noted: his faith was concerned with miracles (13, 19, 20), and ended in amazement, not holiness; his view of God was materialistic. 'Simony' became a term for traffic in sacred things. Gehazi is the Old Testament parallel and perhaps Balaam (2 Pet. ii. 15); his aim was self-aggrandizement; he was afraid (24), but not visibly repentant. Simon disappears at this point from the story, but in legend he has a lurid career of magic and wizardry. Peter's words (23) are the key to Luke's emphasis on the story, and a 'root of bitterness' (Dt. xxix. 18) Simon's tribe have indeed been in the Church.

The Samaritan church found frank acceptance in Jerusalem (25), an outstanding testimony to the new spirit which was abroad. Jewish pride was on the altar.

The admirably-told story of the Ethiopian is probably in Philip's own words, passed on to the author when he and Paul were entertained in the evangelist's house at Caesarea, twenty years later (xxi. 8). As a piece of narrative it ranks with the stories of the Lord's own personal work (e.g. John iii and iv). The following points should be noted:

1. The chain of historical circumstance may have gone back a thousand years. The faith of which Israel was the guardian followed the trade of Solomon and brought the Queen of Sheba from Southern Arabia to Palestine. Southern Arabia and Ethiopia were closely connected with trade in those days, and it is noteworthy that the stock of legend which collected round the persons of Solomon and Sheba's queen had ramifications which involved Ethiopia. Judging from the gifts they brought, the Magi of the Christmas story came from Arabia Felix, Sheba's land, and both they and Candace's chamberlain may indicate that a spark of Messianic expectation had been kept alive over the centuries among 'the devout' of distant lands. All this is speculation, but the 'undergrowth of history' is sometimes a rewarding study.

2. The great geographer of Palestine, Sir George Adam Smith,[1] discusses the 'desert Gaza' (26). It lay on the old strategic route to Egypt, a locality destined to form a nodal point of strife, as ancient and modern history abundantly demonstrate. Hence, too, the fact that it was a posting-station on the Ethiopian's way home. He had no occasion to pass through the sea-port, the 'new' Gaza, by which the Romans had sought to provide a haven for ships on that perennially harbourless coast.

3. The 'angelology' of Acts is discussed by R. B. Rackham.[2] His conclusion is that verse 26 speaks rather of a compelling intuition than of an external visitation. Compare verse 29. Similarly verse 39 probably involves no supernatural removal, but rather a prompt withdrawal on the urge of a strong compulsion. Azotus, the old Philistine stronghold of Ashdod, was not far away.

4. The story sets the seal of New Testament authority on the

[1] *The Historical Geography of the Holy Land*, p. 186.
[2] *Op. cit.*, pp. 71, 72

interpretation of Isaiah liii and the associated 'servant' passages as prophecies of Christ. There is an eloquent chapter on the subject in Sir George Adam Smith's study of Isaiah.[1]

5. The RV, on the strength of compelling MS authority, has removed verse 37 to the margin. It is most unlikely that it does not represent a genuine testimony taken at baptism, but it is the business of the Lower Criticism to discover and accept what the writer originally wrote, and neither to add to nor take away from it. R. B. Rackham's[2] suggestion is likely: '. . . we can imagine that Luke, when revising his work, in his effort after conciseness, drew his pen through it.' An author's erasure can easily account for a strong textual case against a logically appropriate but critically apparent intrusion.

6. Details in the story which may seem odd in a modern context, are perfectly natural, indeed marks of authenticity, in the ancient setting. The Ethiopian, for example, would have been travelling with a considerable company, and it was accepted practice for a lonely stranger to attach himself to a caravan. After the ancient fashion he was reading aloud.

Additional Notes

vii. 20 and 34. Those interested in language, and the evidence of authentic reporting which may sometimes be deduced from linguistic phenomena, should note revealing Hebraisms in these verses. *Exceeding fair* is literally 'fair in the eyes of God', a Greek dative of reference. This renders a Hebrew mode of expression indicating a high degree of the quality of the adjective. Nineveh for example was a city 'great to God' (Jon. iii. 2). *I have seen, I have seen* (34) renders the Greek 'having seen I have seen', which is another Greek attempt to represent the emphatic use of the infinitive absolute in Hebrew noted above on iv. 17.

vii. 38. AV *church* is incorrect. The use is rather political than ecclesiastical, and *ekklēsia* here bears its Greek connotation of

---

[1] Isaiah in the *Expositor's Bible* (Eerdmans' 1956 edition), III, pp. 799 ff. See also F. F. Bruce, *op. cit.*, pp. 193, 194.
[2] *Op. cit.*, p. 123.

'assembly'. It views Israel, assembled at Mt. Sinai, through the eyes of Greek city organization.

vii. 58. *Young man* is a term available for people up to the age of forty. Paul was probably at the time between thirty and forty years of age.

Some numerical discrepancies in chapter vii are of the sort which once provided 'contradictions' for the Ingersoll school of Biblical criticism. It is obvious that Stephen could hardly have risked mistakes before his learned audience. Tradition was wider and fuller than the Old Testament story, as it has come down to us. This is one clear lesson of the Dead Sea Scrolls. In verse 4, and the parallel references in Genesis, there are difficulties over numbers which suggest different readings in older texts which Stephen knew, but which no longer exist.[1] Verse 6 agrees with Gn. xv. 13, but Ex. xii. 40 says 430. Stephen has given a round number, like Josephus. Verse 14 says 75 as against the 70 of Ex. i. 5. This was an ancient variation between the Septuagint and the Hebrew text as we know it. A Qumran version of Exodus from the Dead Sea Scrolls, antedating the standardization of the Hebrew text by two centuries, agrees with the Septuagint in reading 75.

V. THE DAMASCUS ROAD (ix. 1–31)

a. The man (ix. 1, 2)

Paul, or Saul to use his Jewish name, was born at Tarsus in Cilicia,[2] a fact which he himself notes with civic pride (xxi. 39). Tarsus was an ancient city, the seat of a provincial governor when Persia ruled, and, in the days of the Greek Syrian kings, the centre of a lumbering and linen industry. During the first century before Christ the city was the home of a philosophical school, a university town, in a word, where the intellectual atmosphere would be coloured by Greek thought.

Tarsus stood, like Alexandria, at a confluence of East and

---

[1] See F. F. Bruce, *op. cit.*, p. 162.
[2] W. M. Ramsay, *The Cities of Saint Paul*, pp. 85–244.

West. The wisdom of the Greeks, and the world-order of Rome, mingled with the good and ill of Oriental mysticism, were deep in its consciousness. A keen-minded Jew, born and bred at Tarsus, would draw the best from more than one world. He would catch the flavour of western thought, and learn to appreciate the Greco-Roman outlook. He was also in touch with the strong bases of his own tradition. For such a man the synagogue would be no place of refuge from an alien society. There is evidence enough of a missionary zeal among such Jews which prepared the way for Christianity. The Greek translation of the Old Testament stands as a monument to their enthusiasm in Alexandria, and we have already observed the fresh and vigorous minds which Stephen and Philip brought to Christian evangelism.

The signs of a Greek education are visible in Paul. Ramsay[1] points to a subtle irony in his work (for example in 1 Cor. i–iv) which is not Jewish. To anyone with an ear for Greek undertones the source is obvious. There is a logic in his mode of argument which was not built in a day, and which was not the fruit of Hebrew mysticism. Paul had the training of a Greek, as well as the stern and formal education of the Hebrew at Gamaliel's feet, among the best of Jerusalem's Pharisees. Nor must the Roman influence be forgotten. The Jews had been in Tarsus since Antiochus Epiphanes' re-foundation in 171 BC,[2] and Paul belonged to that minority which held the Roman citizenship. 'There is much in a name', writes Ramsay,[3] 'and it is peculiarly unfortunate that no one ever thinks of Paul by his Roman name. But it is as certain that he had a Roman name and spoke the Latin language, as it is that he was a Roman citizen.' It was his appreciation of the Roman concept of empire, as Ramsay shows in the same admirable essay, which led Paul to his master-plan of evangelism. He was, in fact, offering the great empire that cement which it mistakenly sought in the worship of the Emperor, and

[1] *The Teaching of Paul in Terms of the Present Day, passim.*

[2] Ramsay, *The Cities of Saint Paul*, pp. 169–186.

[3] *Pauline Studies*, p. 65. See also pp. 99, 100, 197, 198, 258, and *The Cities of Saint Paul*, pp. 205–214.

which it accepted only when it was too late to save great portions of the imperial structure from disintegration.

Paul was a Pharisee, and something has already been said about this famous order.[1] The rigid upholders of tradition, formalists, a close-knit body with vested interests in the maintenance of Judaism, opponents of enthusiasm, innovation, and unorthodoxy, and, in one scathing speech of Christ Himself, hypocrites who made a show of high sanctity and denied in life and conduct the realities of religion, the Pharisees haunt the background of the New Testament.

Men like Nicodemus and Gamaliel show a better side of the picture, and give some notion of what Pharisees could be, and what, perhaps, they once predominantly were. The part they had once played in purging and preserving Judaism was salutary and noble, but, as so often happens in the institutions of men, sincerity gave place to formalism, and zeal for the Law degenerated into a passion for legality. Rigidity breeds pride, and pride destroys sincerity. Learning goes sour when it loses contact with life, and religion itself, losing its spirit, becomes a closed preserve, the exclusive province of the privileged, jealously fenced. Hence the monumental elaborations of the Law, and the casuistry which made the Law a peril to true religion. Paul should be ranked with his teacher rather than with the casuists. It was from Gamaliel that he drew his great knowledge of the Law. The less reputable Pharisaism of the wing which drew near to the Sadducees made Paul the persecutor.

A few details of biographical interest may be culled from the New Testament. The possession of Roman citizenship, for example, presupposes a family of some wealth and position. So, too, does Paul's nephew's inside knowledge of the priestly plot, and the quite evident respect which the senior Roman officer in Jerusalem paid to the young man (xxiii. 16–22). Paul's sister must have had the best of connections in Jerusalem. A strong suggestion of poverty, on the other hand, argues a deep rift with his family (2 Cor. xi. 8, 9; Phil. iii. 8, iv. 15;

[1] Introduction, pp. 36 ff. above.

1 Thes. ii. 9). Perhaps words like those in Eph. vi. 4 and Col. iii. 21 point back to a searing memory of parental repudiation.

A few hints only in the narrative enable us to picture Paul. We can visualize his orator's gesture of the hands (xiii. 16, xx. 34, xxi. 40, xxvi. 1). There is also a suggestion of an intense gaze, though it must be admitted that the expression is used also of Peter. (See xiii. 9, xiv. 9, xxiii. 1; of Peter, iii. 4; of the congregation in the Capernaum synagogue, Lk. iv. 20.) The word *atenizō* implies a sharp, intent gaze. Ramsay[1] remarks: 'The theory which makes Paul a permanent sufferer in his eyes, unable to see distinctly persons quite near to him, repulsive to strangers ... (Gal. iv. 13, 14), is hopelessly at variance with the facts.' He argues very convincingly[2] that the 'thorn in the flesh' was Asiatic malaria. Of Paul's mind we know the logic (Romans), the poetry (1 Cor. xiii), the ardour (Ephesians), the exquisite tact (Philippians), the eloquence and sheer power.

It has been plausibly suggested[3] that the zeal Paul showed at the time of Stephen's death led to his election to the Sanhedrin, and that he therefore had a judicial part to play in the later stages of the persecution. Perhaps it was from a desire to justify his role that Paul sought to be appointed chief inquisitor at Damascus. From Acts xxvi. 10 we learn that before the journey he had been armed with considerable authority in Jerusalem, and that his vote was active in condemnation of the Sanhedrin's victims. Outwardly, at any rate, he still stood where he stood on the day of Stephen's death. The *high priest* (1) had no authority over the Damascus synagogues, but armed with his prestige Paul, or Saul as he should still be called in this context, could instigate the local rabbis to exercise a discipline, and to hand suspects over to the mercies of the Sanhedrin. It seems clear that the Damascus Christians had not broken with the synagogue. They were

---

[1] *St. Paul the Traveller and Roman Citizen*, p. 39.

[2] *Ibid.*, pp. 94–97.

[3] J. R. Lumby, *op. cit.*, p. 189.

dubbed the people of the *way* (2), a name which reflects their preaching of 'a way of salvation' and their quoting of a saying of the Lord (Jn. xiv. 6).

b. The conversion (ix. 3-9)

There were two roads to Damascus. One was the caravan route from Egypt which followed the coast of Palestine until it struck east to cross the Jordan north of the Lake of Tiberias. To join this road Saul would have first turned westward to the sea. The other way led through Neapolis, crossed the Jordan south of the Lake of Tiberias, passed through Gadara, and ran north-east to Damascus.[1] Somewhere on one of these two roads Saul had that vision of Christ which changed his life, and altered the course of world history. It was conversion, shattering and sudden, and an act of God. Two views of what may be described as the spiritual machinery are held:

1. *Sudden impact.* Ramsay[2] believes that Saul's whole mind and conduct were based on the certainty that the impostor was dead. If that were not so, the whole foundation crumbled beneath his feet. Then, in the mid-course of his mad career, he saw Jesus, so clearly, so unmistakably, that he could not disbelieve. He saw; he heard; he knew; and there was no alternative to surrender.

Two points may be noted. First, Ramsay seems the only leading authority to hold this position. Second, God does not usually deal thus with men. In His grace He sometimes reveals truth with special clarity, but not to complete and implacable hostility; only to bewilderment, however despairing, and to nascent conviction, however overlaid, repressed and beaten down.

2. *Consummation.* Few conversions take place 'out of the blue'. S. H. Mellone[3] writes: 'The moment of a conversion may seem quite sudden and unexpected; but experience shows

---

[1] *Ibid.*, pp. 190, 191.
[2] *The Teaching of Paul in Terms of the Present Day*, pp. 23-28.
[3] *The Bearings of Psychology on Religion*, pp. 154, 155.

that such a fundamental and abrupt occurrence always has a long period of unconscious "incubation". . . . Let us observe again the case of that conversion which changed the history of the world. St. Paul had for long been deeply impressed by his experience of the devotion of the Christians whom he persecuted. Perhaps it would not be going too far to say that he had already been a Christian for a long time but unconsciously; and just for that reason his fanaticism against the Christians increased; for in personalities of this type, fanaticism exists as a compensation for, and in conflict with, secret doubts.' A. F. W. Blunt[1] agrees. 'His furious purpose of persecution', he writes, 'would not be psychologically incompatible with the disquietude of conscience, which a sincere and eager man may feel only the more strongly because he tries to silence it by zealous energy of action.' So does F. W. Farrar[2] in his venerable study of 1884: 'If haunting doubts could for a moment thrust themselves into his thoughts, the vehement self-assertion of contempt would sweep them out, and they would be expiated by fresh zeal against the seductive glamour of the heresy which thus dared to insinuate itself like a serpent into the very hearts of its avengers.' The Dean continues to describe the week-long journey to Damascus, Saul's lonely meditation, alone with memories, the pressure of conscience, the Spirit of God, and the challenge of the Word. R. B. Rackham[3] may be ranged with the same commentators. He writes: 'The voice added, "It is hard for thee to kick against the pricks." This is a common proverb found in Greek and Latin literature, as well as Hebrew; . . . it is thoroughly in the proverbial style, familiar, but incisive, of Jesus of Nazareth. And, in fact, it was the best description of what Saul had been doing—trying to stifle the pricks of his inmost heart of conscience, which all the time was asking, "Is this righteousness of mine own really joy and peace? What if Stephen and the Nazarenes are right after all . . .?" '

[1] *Op. cit.*, p. 170.
[2] *The Life and Work of Saint Paul*, p. 102.
[3] *Op. cit.*, p. 130.

J. S. Stewart[1] devotes a chapter to the theme. He takes the proverb which is twice quoted (ix. 5, xxvi. 14), with its vivid picture of the recalcitrant animal which, as it is being yoked to the plough, kicks out at the man behind it and only hurts itself in doing so, and lists 'the pricks' in first-class homiletic style. Thus there was, first, Saul's own growing sense of the failure of Judaism. His religion had not brought him peace with God. 'Hence the fury of his attack on the new sect. Action might relieve his brooding . . .' Then there was the fact of the historic Jesus. The Pharisees had watched the Lord's ministry carefully. As an honest man Saul could not brush aside the evidence of something extraordinary. Third, he had to account for the lives of the Christians, and, fourth, there was the death of Stephen.

The last point should be emphasized. Luke is a consummate historian, to be ranged in his own right with the great writers of the Greeks. When he makes pointed mention of Saul, and the part he played at the martyr's death, he was deliberately linking Stephen with Saul. He was, after all, the apostle's intimate friend, and knew his mind as no other men. It may safely be deduced from his hint (vii. 58), together with the apostle's own cryptic reference (xxii. 20), that the dying words of Stephen and the manner of his passing were a haunting memory, and that the brilliant speech, which had but stirred the murderous animosity of the Jerusalem Pharisees, gripped the mind of the Jew of Tarsus with strange power.

Remember, finally, the intervention of God. Hostile critics have sought to dismiss the vision of Christ as the hallucination of an epileptic. Ramsay[2] discusses this absurdity, and his argument may be summed up in a quotation: 'There have been madmen at all times; but the difficulty which many feel in classing St. Paul among them arises from the fact that not merely did he persuade every one who heard him that he was sane and spoke the truth, but that also he has moved the world, changed the whole course of history, and made us what

[1] *A Man in Christ*, pp. 119–141.
[2] *Pauline Studies*, chapter i.

we are. Is the world moved at the word of a lunatic? To think so would be to abandon all belief in the existence of order and unity in the world and in history; and therefore we are driven to the conclusion that St. Paul's vision is one of those things about which evidence ought to be examined without any foregone conclusion in the mind.' Suffice it to add to Ramsay's reserved words that the apostle's life, half the New Testament, and all European history, together with all the history and thought derived therefrom, is evidence.

Saul was converted. He was to be Paul, the apostle to the Gentiles. He was already near middle age, with the vast task of the world's evangelization ahead of him. God seemed in no hurry. Fourteen years, over which Luke passes, are mentioned by Paul (Gal. i. 15–ii. 1) as his period of preparation. Probably the earliest acceptable date for the conversion on the Damascus road is AD 33. This would leave AD 33–46 for the visit to Arabia (Gal. i. 17) and the restoration of the man after the shattering experience he had known, and for the early ministry in Tarsus, Syria, Cilicia, and Antioch, which prepared mind and method for the major assault on the pagan world. The splendid deliberateness with which God forged His human tool is the great lesson of these years. Impatient men forget that God is not bound by time. His conversion was by far the most vital influence in Paul's life. Ancestry, Pharisaic training, Hellenistic education, were fused by it into the character which the Holy Spirit formed and fashioned over the fourteen years of training. At length, in God's good time, the door opened, and the events of half a lifetime assumed final and complete significance. So often with man's days in Christ. The traveller breasts a last rise, looks back and sees the road behind, the reason for its bends and turnings, and its unerring movement to a goal. And in the vision the crooked places become straight and the rough places plain.

c. The sequel (ix. 10–31)

Luke is approaching that part of his narrative in which the apostle to the Gentiles steps to the forefront of the stage, and

Peter retires from view. He has held the plan of his book consciously in mind from the beginning. His significant introduction of the Hellenistic Jews has been observed, and the glimpses he has shown of the wider world into which the gospel was to move in the ministry of Paul. He has now told us of Paul's conversion, and intends, before moving on to the account of Paul's missionary journeys, and those events whereby the global purport of the gospel was realized, to write of Peter's call to a wider evangelism.

Chapters ix and x therefore cohere and form a twofold and powerful introduction to that which is to follow. The two great leaders are shown side by side, united before a major task, and in significant rebuttal of the attempts of those who, in the ancient and the modern world, with mischievous tongue or irresponsible pen, have sought to divide them. Conybeare and Howson[1] remark on the symmetry with which Luke sets forth the two stories: 'The simultaneous preparation of the hearts of Ananias and of Saul, and the simultaneous preparation of those of Peter and Cornelius,—the questioning and hesitation of Peter and the questioning and hesitation of Ananias,—the one doubting whether he might make friendship with the Gentiles, the other doubting whether he might approach the enemy of the Church,—the unhesitating obedience of each when the Divine will was made known,—the state of mind in which both the Pharisee and the centurion were found,—each waiting to see what the Lord would say to them,—this close analogy will not be forgotten by those who reverently read the two consecutive chapters. . . .' Perversely to see such parallelism as a mark of fiction is to take small account of the literary methods of the ancient world.

In 2 Cor. xi. 32, 33 Paul later amplifies the story of his escape from Damascus (24, 25). It was a complex of events with which he was to become painfully familiar over the next twenty years—a challenging gospel, Jewish resentment, the crystallizing of that resentment into organized violence, the enlistment of civic authority, and precarious escape.

[1] *The Life and Epistles of Saint Paul*, p. 77 (*sic punct.*).

A knotty historical problem[1] is involved in the position of
Aretas (see 2 Cor. xi. 32), and the sphere of jurisdiction in
which Damascus lay at the time of the Jewish attack. It seems
likely that the synagogue authorities took advantage of some
change in local government which favoured their plot. In
Jerusalem, history was repeated (29), with Paul ranged,
ironically enough, against a group of Hellenistic Jews. These
Hellenistic Jews (AV, *Grecians*) were those at whose instigation
Stephen had been murdered. Lumby[2] remarks that the same
word is used for Paul's 'disputing' as was employed in the
description of the controversies (vi. 9) which Stephen's ministry occasioned. Nor is the verb found elsewhere in the book.
But the attack is now reversed with Paul holding the initiative.
The 'Grecians' disputed with Stephen. The superbly educated
Pharisee disputes with them.

Additional Notes

ix. 2. Literally '. . . if he should find any of "the Way".' A
note of contempt for the Christian's familiar quotation is in the
phrase. It is of course a natural enough metaphor for a religion
involving a code of moral conduct, and occurs in more than
one language. Our 'way of life' is, after all, identical. See xix.
9, 23, xxii. 4, xxiv. 14, 22 (and cf. xvi. 17, xviii. 25, 26; 2 Pet.
ii. 2).

ix. 4. Commentators note the Hebrew form of the vocative,
with its suggestion of well-remembered address. So too,
appropriately, in verse 17 (and in xxii. 7, 13, xxvi. 14).

ix. 7. This does not contradict xxii. 9. The verb 'to hear' in
Greek can govern an accusative (xxii. 9) or a genitive (ix. 7).
The genitive is partitive and in itself conveys the idea that they
did not apprehend the sound in its entirety. Hence the genitive
at ix. 7. It was correct to use the accusative in the second
context. The accusative signifies a complete domination of the
object, and the company did not understand the purport of

---

[1] *Knowling, op. cit.,* II, p. 240 for details and relevant authorities.
[2] *Op. cit.,* p. 203.

the words. Admittedly this distinction is often blurred, but Luke is a careful writer. Moulton remarks of this passage: 'The fact that the maintenance of an old and well-known distinction between the acc. and gen. with *akouō* saves the author of Acts ix. 7 and xxii. 9 from a patent self-contradiction, should by itself be enough to make us recognise it for Luke and for other writers until it is proved wrong.'[1]

ix. 9. It is reasonably suggested that these *three days* were the occasion of the experiences of 2 Cor. xii. 1–4.

ix. 18. Commentators point out that Luke uses the term for *scales* employed by Hippocrates, and that the cognate verb is found in the rather horrible account of blindness and healing in the book of Tobit (iii. 17, xi. 13). But surely there is nothing highly technical in the word and the expression need not be literal. There fell '*as it had been* scales', and Luke was certainly speaking metaphorically.

ix. 19. *Certain days* is a Lucan formula for a very brief period of time (x. 48, xv. 36, xvi. 12, xxiv. 24, xxv. 13).

VI. PETER USES THE KEYS (ix. 32–xii. 25)

a. Lydda (ix. 32–35)

Near Lydda, according to early Christian tradition, Saint George slew the dragon. The connection between this tale and the Greek myth of Perseus, who also slew a scaly monster on this coast and thereby saved Andromeda, is a problem for the students of legend-lore. Both dragon and monster probably preserve a folk-memory of the Philistine fish-god, Dagon, worshipped of old in nearby Ashdod. 'If the derivation be correct,' writes Sir George Adam Smith,[2] 'it is a curious process by which the monster, symbolic of heathenism conquered by Christianity, has been evolved out of the first great rival of Christianity. And could there be a fitter scene for such a legend

---

[1] *Prolegomena* to his *Grammar of New Testament Greek*, p. 66.
[2] *The Historical Geography of the Holy Land*, p. 164.

than the town where Hebrew touched Philistine, Jew struggled with Greek, and Christendom contested with Islam.'

The ancient Philistine territory on the maritime plain was, in New Testament times, a stronghold of Jewry.[1] Peter was about his proper business as an apostle to the Jews, when he paid the congregation of Lydda the visit here recorded. He was also performing the species of episcopal function which he exercised in the case of Samaria. It was a visit to confirm the converts of Philip, and to inspect the work done in the area. In both the case of Samaria and of Lydda, Luke mentions the visit casually, and as a preliminary to the important narrative of Joppa. Note, too, that the case of Aeneas and that of Tabitha are mentioned, each in its place, to provide contemporary authentication of Peter's ministry. It was important to demonstrate that Peter was in the full stream of his usefulness, and the agent of miracles curiously like those performed by his Master (Mt. ix. 23–26; Mk. v. 38–43; Jn. v. 6–9), when the call came to him to baptize a Gentile.

b. Joppa (ix. 36–x. 23)

i. Tabitha (ix. 36–43). The story of Tabitha is simply and vividly told, and is full of circumstantial detail. The following should be noted. First, the burial customs. Outside Jerusalem a body might be kept unburied for three days and three nights. In Jerusalem, as illustrated by the case of Ananias and Sapphira, no corpse lay overnight. Second, the natural feminine touch in verse 39. The verb is middle suggesting that the widows were wearing the garments they showed to Peter. Third, the circumstantial details of the woman's gradual recovery in verses 40 and 41.

Strict Jewry held the trade of a *tanner* (43) as unclean, because of the constant handling of dead animals it necessarily involved. The fact that Peter is found at the close of this chapter lodging with Simon the tanner, indicates that a measure of Jewish prejudice was already banished from his thinking. We have noticed the subtlety with which Luke

[1] Knowling, *op. cit.*, II, p. 245, quotes relevant authorities.

suggested Paul's mental preparation for the catastrophic experience of chapter ix. With similar significance the closing verse of the chapter prepares the way for the narrative of chapter x. Indeed reflection upon his position and the calling of his host may have provided the raw material for Peter's dream.

ii. Peter's vision (x. 1–23). Cornelius was one of the multitude of Gentiles who had been attracted to Judaism. Such allegiance crops up in many odd corners of surviving literature. A member of the Flavian family, for example, was accused of 'going astray after the customs of the Jews',[1] and Juvenal writes with scorn of one who accepts Jewish food taboos and circumcision,

> *And, taught the Roman ritual to deride,*
> *Clings to the Jewish, and observes with awe*
> *All Moses bade in his mysterious law.*
> *And therefore to the circumcised alone*
> *Will point the road or make the fountain known.*[2]

For all the contempt of Roman satirists and historians, an earnest minority of dissatisfied pagans had found in the Septuagint and the synagogue a satisfaction for the soul denied them in the state cults and mystery religions. We meet them repeatedly in the New Testament, and again and again find them ripe for the message of the gospel, and free by nature from those inhibitions which made it so difficult for the Jews to see beyond a national religion (cf. xiii. 16, 26, 43, 50, xvi. 14, xvii. 4, 17, xviii. 7).

The kindly tanner had made his guest comfortable on the roof, and had spread a leather awning, hung by its four corners over his couch. Dinner tarried, and Peter, weary from his wayfaring, fell asleep at prayer. The situation is touchingly human. The last impress on the tired man's drowsy mind was the drooping awning, and the sky at its four sides. Out of such homely stuff was fashioned the imagery of the dream which was to have historic consequences.

[1] Dion Cassius, LXVII. 44.
[2] *Satires*, XIV. 96–105. Horace, Pliny the Elder, Tacitus and Suetonius might be similarly quoted.

The story is convincingly told with an economy of language in Luke's best style. Peter's protest is strongly characteristic, and the divine reply curiously similar in tone to more than one rebuke provoked by the impulsive disciple in the days of his Master.[1] The threefold repetition might also remind Peter of an interview on a familiar beach.[2] The vision was built of the simplicities of life, but was divinely authenticated. If any doubt remained, it was dispelled by the visitors at Simon's gate and the command to accompany them.

c. Caesarea (x. 24-48)

At the headquarters of the Palestinian command Peter meets Cornelius. Note a singular feature of Luke's style. He is ruthless in his brevity when he narrates events without immediate significance in the plan of his story. He is prepared for repetition when he is setting forth important movements in the record. We shall note the same phenomenon in the next chapter, and in the triple repetition of the story of Paul's conversion.

Note the full Christology of Peter's speech. Peter was the first to declare that Jesus was the Messiah, and in his exposition of the gospel to his Gentile audience he covers the same theme fully and faithfully. Peter and Paul, remarks R. J. Knowling,[3] 'are both one in their witness to the Resurrection of the Christ on the third day, and also in their witness to His appointment as the future Judge of mankind. This startling claim made by St. Peter with reference to Jesus of Nazareth, with whom he had lived on terms of closest human intimacy, and in whose death he might well have seen the destruction of all his hopes, is a further evidence of the change which could only be accounted for by the belief that this same Jesus was risen, and declared to be the Son of God with power.'

The speaking *with tongues* of verse 46 was probably the Corinthian phenomenon of ecstatic utterance. Nonetheless this

---

[1] Mt. xvi. 22; Jn. xiii. 8.
[2] Jn. xxi. 17.
[3] *Op. cit.*, II, p. 261.

event may rightly be described as the Gentile Pentecost. Notice that the manifest presence of the Holy Spirit preceded baptism. Peter, it is noted, *commanded them to be baptized* (48). He refrained from personally baptizing the converts in accordance, no doubt, with an apostolic practice designed to prevent factions. (See Paul's remarks in 1 Cor. i. 13–16.)

d. Jerusalem (xi. 1–18)

This passage is a strong light on the nature and preoccupations of the Jerusalem church, and the situation with which Paul was later to contend. It is clear that Christianity was accepted as a reformed Judaism, and not Judaism's successor. True, the assembly accepts Peter's explanation, and gave God glory (18), but it is clear from the outcome that they could have contemplated little more than that type of spiritual hospitality which the synagogues, especially those of the Dispersion, had long offered to the God-fearing among the Gentiles. It was a different matter when Paul threw the Church open to all Gentiles, whether they had previously conformed to Judaism or not. Probably, too, as A. W. F. Blunt suggests,[1] 'such is human nature, they may have thought that such cases as that of Cornelius were likely to be few and exceptional, before the Return of Jesus took place, and that a minority of Gentiles on the circumference of the Church might be tolerated, especially as they might possibly in time go on to be circumcised through the influence of the Jewish majority.' It required, indeed, a major readjustment of all thinking for a people, fiercely conscious of racial privilege and stirred anew by the thought that the Messiah of promise had appeared and spoken, readily to abandon the thought that a unique national destiny approached fulfilment. To accept a re-interpretation of ancient prophecies, to admit a spiritual rendering of old promises accepted and cherished as literal and material, to see Israel melt into the Church, and the minority of the chosen lose identity, privilege, and special place in a global organization, called for insight, faith, self-abnegation, magnanimity, and a

[1] *Op. cit.*, p. 179.

transcendent view of God rarely found in any but the most enlightened souls. We see Paul occasionally waver. We sense the struggle of Peter towards the wider vision, and we shall see him falter in the difficult path. It is easy to dismiss the prejudices of the Jerusalem church as narrow-minded and un-Christian; but it is better to look upon such 'agonizing reappraisal' with a sympathetic eye, and to appreciate the greatness of the men who rose to the occasion, and especially of that mighty spirit towards whose work the story is tending.

e. The wider world (xi. 19-30)

The story of Peter's imprisonment in chapter xii is a continuation of the 'acts' which began in chapter x. Luke's purpose, therefore, in introducing this interlude must be sought. He was probably intent on drawing some threads of narrative together, and showing that, while significant events were taking place in the citadels of Jewry, there was a ferment abroad in the great centres of the Gentile world, and that while Peter was being prepared for his role of leadership in Jerusalem, God's time was ripening for the introduction of Saul of Tarsus to the task of Gentile evangelism. The mention of the collection (27-30) is relevant to this end, for that obligation was to be a major occasion of liaison between the Gentile and Jewish sections of the Church, and a link between the apostle to the Gentiles and Jerusalem Jewry. The section is also designed to show that the Jerusalem church was not without a sense of responsibility towards the world at large, nor without wisdom in its choice of an officer to report on spiritual developments there (22). Barnabas is one of the choice saints of the early Church, a man of insight, willing to move others to the forefront of the stage, gracious and wise. He it was who had first sponsored Saul, and now, seeing the whitening fields of the Gentile world, he thinks of his one-time protégé and brings him to Antioch (26). No doubt at Barnabas' suggestion the same Saul is appointed to visit Jerusalem under circumstances calculated to find him acceptance there (30).

f. Jerusalem again (xii. 1–19)

Herod Agrippa 1, grandson of Herod called 'the Great', had grown up in imperial circles in Rome. He was a friend of the third emperor, the mad Caligula, and had contrived to aid Caligula's successor, Claudius, in the vital matter of his elevation to the principate. Hence the addition of Judaea and Samaria to the territory which Caligula had granted him. This was the tetrarchy of Philip (Lk. iii. 1), later extended by the further assignment of Galilee and Peraea, the old domain of Herod Antipas. The title of 'king' accompanied Caligula's appointment. Notorious in Rome for his prodigality and extravagance, in Judaea Herod posed as a champion of the Law. The attack on the Church was no doubt a policy move to gratify and conciliate the old Pharisaic and Sadducean enemies of the Church.

The persecution, therefore, and the imprisonment of Peter recorded in this chapter, follow in direct sequence the events narrated in x. 1–xi. 18. The zealous observance, which had heretofore marked the Jerusalem church, had gone far to allay the fears of the religious leaders. Provided Christianity remained within the strict Jewish fold, and confined its activities to the framework of the old faith, the Sadducees had no fault to find with it, and the Pharisees found no cause for complaint. But Peter's report caused alarm which spread beyond the confines of the Church. Vested interests took fright, and, either directly persuaded, or sensing an opportunity, the king started his petty persecution.

The narrative of Peter's imprisonment and deliverance bears all the freshness and vividness of a first-hand account. Peter himself, and John Mark, in whose mother's house (12) the very human little drama of verses 13 to 16 was enacted, were close enough to the story of this book and to its writer. Where Peter hid is not known. There seems to be no evidence for a retreat to Rome, and Luke had his own reasons for the lack of detail. He is preparing to usher Peter from the stage, as Paul steps to the forefront. The apostle to the Jews has played his part. He has, in fact, prepared the way for the apostle to the

Gentiles, and it was not within Luke's present plan to say more of him. It is the world's loss that he did not write a third account for his friend Theophilus, continuing the unfinished narrative of Acts, and recounting other apostolic ministries.

g. Caesarea again (xii. 20–25)

It is appropriate that the chapter should end with the story of the death of the persecutor. Josephus, who looked with favour on Herod, gives a much longer account of his passing.[1] It was a case of what the Greeks would have called 'hybris', that fatal sin of the spirit whereby man, lifting himself beyond man's allotted elevation, invites and calls down the judgment of heaven. The Greeks would have agreed whole-heartedly with Luke that Herod died for this species of blasphemy. For those who are curious about the natural mechanism of the judgment which fell upon the king, Dr. A. Rendle Short[2] has a convincing diagnosis, rather more gruesome in its patient detail than the briefer account given in verse 23 by his fellow-doctor, Luke.

Additional Notes

ix. 35. Calvin has a sensible note on this verse. 'When the Scripture saith *all*, it doth not comprehend every one, however so many it noteth, but it putteth *all* for the more part, or for many, or for the common sort of men.' For language similarly Eastern in its hyperbole, cf. Gn. xli. 54, 57; Dt. ii. 25; Jb. xxxvii. 3; Lk. ii. 1; Acts ii. 25; Rom. i. 8, etc.

x. 1. An inscription from Austria dated AD 69 contains the abbreviated words: OPT. COH. II ITAL. C.R.F. . . . TINI EX VEXIL. SAGIT. EXER. SYR., i.e. adjutant of the second Italian cohort of Roman citizens, of the century of Faustinus, from the archery division of the army of Syria.

x. 28. The word translated *of another nation* is used nowhere else in the New Testament. It marks Peter's tact. There

---

[1] *Ant. Jud.* xix. 8. 2.
[2] *The Bible and Modern Medicine*, pp. 66–68.

is no suggestion of inferiority which other words for Gentiles might have contained.

x. 33. The AV is a little austere. Translate: 'It was good of you to come.'

x. 34. 'Truly', says Peter, '*I am laying hold* of the truth that God is no respecter of persons.' The verb is a strong one. It is used in Jn. i. 5 ('the darkness did not *lay hold* of it'); Rom. ix. 30 ('. . . have *laid hold* on righteousness'); Phil. iii. 12 ('. . . if I may but *lay hold* . . . the Lord *laid hold* of me').

xi. 18. An inferential particle, used in the concluding sentence, points to the surprised realization of something which has been true but unrecognized for some time: 'Then to the Gentiles also has God granted repentance unto life.'

xi. 28. See above on ix. 35 for the expression 'throughout the whole world'. Ramsay[1] shows that *oikoumenē*, the word here used, means the organized Roman world. It is historical fact that the principate of Claudius saw wide-spread shortages throughout the Roman world. In fact Nature in the whole Mediterranean area was beginning to hit back. For too many centuries men had mined the soil, and denuded its hills of a saving forest-covering. Crises of infertility were arising, and notable encroachments of the desert on the sown.

xii. 15. It was the Jewish belief that each individual was under the care of a guardian angel (cf. Mt. xviii. 10; Heb. i. 14). The statement in Tobit v. 21 which promises that 'a good angel' shall accompany the hero's pilgrimage is, according to Rackham, the first reference to this belief.

VII. THE FIRST JOURNEY (xiii. 1–xiv. 26)

a. Antioch (xiii. 1–3)

The concluding paragraph of chapter xi was designed to prepare the way for the narrative of Paul's first missionary

[1] *Was Christ Born at Bethlehem?* pp. 118 f.

journey. The world ministry which thus began was destined to change the history of Europe and the world. Its record begins with the curiously simple and matter-of-fact words of xiii. 1-3. Antioch was the second great metropolis of the Church and the mother of Gentile Christianity. It was an important city, the Roman headquarters of Syria and Cilicia, the location of the imperial mint, and the cosmopolitan meeting-place of Jew, Greek, Roman, and Syrian. Here Christianity first encountered the full broad stream of the Empire's varied life. Here the faith first attracted pagan attention. The Antiochenes were notorious for their dubbing of nicknames, and it was among them that 'the disciples were first called Christians' (xi. 26). Since the name was a Latin formation it may have been an invention of the official archivist. It reoccurs twice, at xxvi. 28, and 1 Pet. iv. 16.

It is implied in xi. 22, 23 that the Jerusalem church was conscious of its seniority. It is interesting to note its spiritual awareness of events in Antioch, and its wisdom in choosing the tactful and broad-minded Barnabas for an official visit and a report. It is possible that this great and choice spirit had first conceived the idea of using for Christ the vast abilities of the converted Pharisee, and it was a wise plan of the Antioch congregation to associate Saul with the delegate from Jerusalem, in the task of carrying thither the contribution for poor-relief (xi. 30). It is implied that Barnabas was responsible for the transference of Saul from Tarsus to Antioch, and the visit to Jerusalem was a necessary prelude to the wider usefulness which Barnabas and far-seeing leaders in Antioch had planned for him.

It is not to be supposed that Saul was unknown in Antioch before Barnabas sought him in Tarsus (xi. 25). Twelve years at least of the future apostle's activity are unaccounted for in Luke's narrative. It is probable that a glimpse is given of the labours of this period in 2 Cor. xi. 24-28. Note the detail: (i) On five occasions he was condemned by Jewish courts. One of these punishments was presumably at Damascus. The rest, if not all, took place during the unrecorded period, and each experience of hostility and rejection was no doubt the usual climax to a long endeavour to bring Christ to the synagogue. (ii) On three occasions he was scourged by Romans. Of these Philippi accounts for only one. (iii) On three occasions Paul was shipwrecked, and this does not include Malta. A very full programme of coastal voyaging in the eastern Mediterranean seems to be demanded. (iv) xi. 26 says Paul remained at Antioch 'a whole year', a remark which suggests something unusual in so long a stay.

b. Cyprus (xiii. 4-12)

The sprawling island in the north-eastern corner of the Mediterranean was an ancient meeting-place of nations. There were large settlements of Jews (xi. 19, 20). Barnabas himself was a Cypriot, and Cypriots had played a part in the founding of the church in Antioch. It was natural that the island should be chosen as the first scene of organized missionary evangelism.

Note the shape of Paul's ministry. He began with the Jews whom he regarded as prepared and privileged by God. Then he passed through the island systematically, from Salamis in the east to Paphos in the south-west. Contact with the Gentiles flowed naturally from the circumstances of his testimony.

Readers with some knowledge of ancient history often have occasion to note Luke's careful writing. Verse 7 is an example. In 22 BC Augustus made Cyprus a senatorial province. That is to say, within the system of disguised autocracy which he had invented, he placed the island under the control of the Senate, instead of retaining it under his own direct authority. It was therefore governed by a proconsul or *deputy* (7). The name of a proconsul called Paulus has been discovered in a North Cypriot inscription.[1] The proconsul of Luke's narrative is described as 'a man of understanding' (7, RV). This is not inconsistent with the presence of a Jewish imposter in his suite. The contemporary Roman was extraordinarily prone to superstition and the 'Chaldaeans and soothsayers', the casters of horoscopes and all manner of associated charlatans, mainly

[1] Details are accessible in Knowling, *op. cit.*, II, p. 286.

from the east, formed a host who battened on this failing. Tacitus[1] describes them as '. . . a tribe faithless to the powerful, deceitful to those who hope, which will ever be banned among us—and ever tolerated.' Juvenal[2] pictures the Emperor Tiberius himself in retirement in Capri 'with his wizard crew'. Sergius Paulus appears to have held his Jewish fortune-teller with a light hand, and to have been convinced by the missionaries' exposure of him.

Whether this conviction involved conversion is not quite clear. Certainly the same word (*believed*) is used in both verses 12 and 48, and the latter case involves conversion. The account is very brief, and to say that one incident is singled out for attention because Peter had a similar experience (viii. 9–13), is not to make a concession to the perverse criticism which sees the New Testament as a scene of rivalry between the two apostles. The proconsul may have had further conversations with Paul (cf. xxiv. 24), and Renan's inability to believe that a person in exalted office could accept the message of the gospel is abundantly refuted by the record of first-century Christianity.[3]

c. Perga (xiii. 13)

The region of Pamphylia seems to have been evangelized only on the return journey (xiv. 25). Yet it might seem logical to expect such a mission on the party's first arrival. Was there a temporary change in plan, and, if so, why? In Gal. iv. 13, Paul, speaking to the churches of South Galatia, the region of Antioch, Iconium, and Derbe, mentions a serious and ravaging illness which was physically apparent on his first visit to them. The climate of the coastal region of Pamphylia is extraordinarily enervating, and after the strain and fatigues of Cyprus, Paul may have fallen a victim to the malaria endemic in the region. Ramsay argues convincingly that this malady, with its penetrating headache and humiliating weakness, was

[1] *Hist.* i. 22.
[2] *Sat.* x. 94.
[3] See James Orr, *Neglected Factors in the Study of the Early Progress of Christianity*, pp. 95–159.

the 'thorn in the flesh' of 2 Cor. xii. 7.[1] The best relief from an attack would be a swift retreat to the highlands north of the Taurus, where Antioch stood at 3,600 feet. The route between Perga and the Pisidian Antioch was arduous and bandit-ridden, with 'perils of robbers' and 'perils of waters' (2 Cor. xi. 26). Either this sudden confrontation of danger, or more worthily, the changed policy of evangelization, working on a rigid, youthful mind, led to a quarrel which Paul remembered painfully for years (xv. 38). John Mark left the party.

d. Antioch in Pisidia (xiii. 14-50)

This city was the chief town of the Roman province of South Galatia.[2] The region was also known as Phrygia. Arriving as strangers in the late summer or autumn of AD 46, Paul and Barnabas took their seats in the synagogue. The lessons may have been Deuteronomy i and Isaiah i,[3] after the reading of which the rulers sent the customary invitation to the visitors to address the gathering. Just as at Philippi (xvi. 13), the events of the first sabbath in a new city are described in some detail.

Luke clearly regards this visit as marking a great turning-point in the apostle's life, and for that reason gives a fairly full report of the address in the synagogue. The style shows a similarity to that of Stephen, not without traces of Peter's manner, but this does not exclude marks of an undoubted Paulinism. The history of the Jewish people, Paul maintains, becomes intelligible only in the consummation found in Christ, in whom the promise, given originally to the Jews, found fulfilment. The Law cannot save; it is incomplete (27, 32, 33, 39). This, of course, is the theme of the Epistle to the Galatians. In spite of God's preparation through all history (17-23), and especially through the ministry of the Fore-runner (24, 25), the Jews of Jerusalem rejected Him (27-29), but in so doing fulfilled prophecy, and set atonement and resurrection in the gospel (30-41).

---

[1] *St. Paul the Traveller and Roman Citizen*, pp. 92-97.
[2] For a full description, geographical, historical, cultural, see W. M. Ramsay, *The Cities of Saint Paul*, III, pp. 247-308.
[3] *Ibid.*, p. 297.

This exposition of the Christian position does not seem to have aroused Jewish opposition in spite of the latent Judaism of the district. It was a remote region, and at this date, through a variety of historical reasons,[1] free from the major prejudices of orthodox Jewry. Timothy, who came from neighbouring Lystra (xvi. 1), was of mixed parentage, and this fact may indicate a certain liberalism in the South Galatian synagogues. What does seem to have stirred animosity is the open extension of the invitation to the Gentiles (45), an historic decision which Luke has in mind when he highlights this chapter (46–49). Like those of Palestine, the Jews of the Dispersion were rejecting Christ. Jewish influence now began to work against the mission. In Asia Minor women enjoyed considerable authority and standing, and it is significant to find them used to persecute Paul and Barnabas. It is also sad, but not without historical and modern parallels, to find *the devout and honourable* (50) ranged against the good.

e. Iconium (xiii. 51–xiv. 5)

The evangelists withdrew ninety miles, and events took a not dissimilar course. Iconium, the Damascus of Asia Minor,[2] was an ancient foundation, rich in history, and prosperous. It was not at this date a Roman colony, but was strongly Romanized, and bore in its population those three elements in which Paul moved at ease, the Jewish, the Greek, and the Roman. Beneath all three was the Anatolian sub-stratum which Paul was to encounter disturbingly at Lystra.

Although Luke chooses to be brief, no doubt because of some similarity between the course of events in Antioch and Iconium, it seems clear that the apostles spent some time in the second city (3), and the success of this longer mission is reflected in later history. Iconium became a major centre for the diffusion of the gospel, and geographical convenience is probably not the only reason for this influence.

The Jewish opposition *stirred up the Gentiles* (2) until *the city*

---

[1] *Ibid.*, pp. 255–259.
[2] Ramsay, *op. cit.*, IV, pp. 317–384, gives a detailed account.

was divided (4). The result was riot condoned by the rulers, and the withdrawal of the apostles from the scene of evidently successful labours.[1]

f. Lystra (xiv. 6–19)

Lystra was an obvious refuge from the troubles of Iconium. It was a Roman colony of Augustus' foundation, with an aristocratic core of Roman citizens, who would be likely to honour Paul's similar status. It was, however, a rustic community, and ranks with Berea, another town of refuge, among the 'cities of Saint Paul'.[2] In xiv. 6 it is implied that, in passing from Iconium to Lystra, the party crossed a frontier. Geographers, basing their contention upon what appeared to be competent ancient authority, once set this statement down as an error on Luke's part. Local inscriptions, obviously more trustworthy than geographers, convinced W. M. Ramsay that the writer of Acts was correct.[3] A writer on Acts has so frequently occasion to quote Ramsay's devoted work that the text assumes exegetical significance. It was the beginning of a series of discoveries which turned Sir William Ramsay into the stout champion of Luke as a Greek historian which he became.

In Lystra, Ramsay found an inscription dedicating a statue to Zeus and Hermes. The two deities are linked in a local cult explained by the Roman poet Ovid, who tells the touching tale of Philemon and Baucis, the Darby and Joan who, in Lycaonia, 'entertained angels unawares'.[4] The two gods, latinized in Ovid and the AV as Jupiter and Mercury, were the deities to whom the enthusiastic Lycaonians likened Paul and Barnabas (12). The accuracy of the background is striking. The belief that the more statuesque and silent of the two

---

[1] A late second-century document, the *Acts of Paul and Thekla*, tells a fictitious story of the Iconium ministry, and among some semi-historical touches it may contain, is a description of Paul, which might or might not have pleased its subject. He was, says the account, 'a man of small size, with meeting eye-brows and rather large nose, bald, bow-legged, full of grace, for at times he looked like a man and at times he had the face of an angel'. [2] Ramsay, *op. cit.*, VI, pp. 407–422.
[3] F. F. Bruce (*op. cit.*, p. 279) collects the evidence.
[4] *Metamorphoses*, viii. 620–724.

figures was the superior (Jupiter) is characteristically Oriental, and an indication of the strength of the Anatolian element beneath the veneer of Hellenism in the town. An inscription has been found at Isauria near Lystra to 'Zeus before the gate'.[1] It may be inferred that the altar was also *before their city* (13) at Lystra, and that the proposed sacrifice was to take place outside the gate. The apostles had probably proceeded to their lodgings after healing the lame man, and when they heard of the preparations for sacrifice hurried forth again.

The old enemies from Antioch and Iconium now arrive on the scene (19), and, after the fickle fashion of crowds, feeling was stirred against the apostles, and a vicious assault staged against Paul. It was not a Jewish stoning, such as that to which Stephen fell a victim, but a piece of mob violence on the part of the Lycaonian natives, egged on by the Jews and mortified by those who had rejected their divine honours. Writing to the same Galatians (vi. 17) Paul states: 'I bear in my body the marks of the Lord Jesus.' He probably won these scars at Lystra. Ramsay points to verse 19 as an example of Luke's historical manner. He contrasts its careful phraseology with the full evidence about the condition of the lame man. In verse 19 he simply states that the persecutors 'supposed Paul to be dead'. Ramsay concludes: 'A writer who tried to find marvels would have found one here, and said so.'[2]

Paul's address, briefly reported in three verses (15–17), the first recorded appeal to a pagan audience, is singularly true to Paul's method. As at Athens (xvii. 24), Paul is found 'laying the foundation of his teaching as a wise master-builder in the truths of natural religion, and leading his audience from them as stepping-stones to higher things.'[3]

g. Derbe (xiv. 20, 21a)

At Derbe,[4] on the limits of the Roman province, the evangelists paused. A few scattered stones on the lonely plain, and

---

[1] See Ramsay, *The Church in the Roman Empire*, p. 51.
[2] *St. Paul the Traveller and Roman Citizen*, p. 120.
[3] R. J. Knowling, *op. cit.*, II, p. 309.
[4] Ramsay, *The Cities of Saint Paul*, v, pp. 385-406.

one or two Christian inscriptions, are the only evidence of life, secular or religious, which once flourished there. Eastern Christians have maintained that the 8,000-foot peak of Hadji-Baba, or the Pilgrim Father, to translate the title, which dominates the empty plain, contains a memory of Saint Paul. Rather say that the Moslem title speaks of the completeness with which the creed of the Turk blotted out a Christian witness. Derbe was one of the least cultured of the cities of Acts and seems to have made little impression on the Church.

h. Back to Syrian Antioch (xiv. 21b–26)

From Derbe the party turned back. The local magistrates had not formally exiled Paul and Barnabas, and would, in any case, now be superseded. It was therefore possible, though no doubt perilous, to return over the old route. Open preaching seems, for obvious reasons, to have been avoided. Instead Paul devoted his energies to establishing the converts in their faith (22), and organizing their communities (23). The basic arrangement seems to have been the appointment of *elders* (23), an eminently sensible scheme, in tune with common secular practice, which in no way interfered with the emergence of gifted leadership of other types, for example, the 'prophets and teachers' of xiii. 1. It became Paul's standard practice (cf. Tit. i. 5). A brief mission was held in Perga (25), where some misfortune prevented their preaching on the outward journey, but this was the only evangelistic task undertaken on the way home. Cyprus was completely omitted. It had been an astonishing year, in many ways one of the most fruitful and varied in Paul's career. Luke has now shown us Peter and Paul being drawn to the joint experience of the following chapter.

Additional Notes

xiii. 1. The pre-eminence of Barnabas is implied by the order of the names in this and the following verse. It occurs again in verse 7, but in verse 13 the phrase is 'Paul and his company', and in Greek such a phrase implies the pre-eminence of the person named.

xiii. 5. Bruce (*op. cit.*, p. 255) remarks that John Mark may have accompanied the party as 'a duly authorized catechist'. He was, of course, a nephew of Barnabas (Col. iv. 10), but Paul, at this stage, may have been eager to have the services of a first-hand witness of the Lord's Passion. Mark's Gospel may have been taking shape at the time.

xiii. 8. No completely satisfactory explanation of the name Elymas (or Etymas, or Etoimas of other MSS), and how it comes to be the 'interpretation' of the sorcerer's name can be given. Ingenious suggestions will be found in the Greek commentaries and elsewhere, but it may be simplest to regard our knowledge of Cypriot Greek as incomplete.

xiii. 21. Saul's 40 years are not mentioned in the Old Testament. Josephus (*Ant.* vi. 14. 9) mentions 20 years, and the total, in any case, may include the judgeship of Samuel. Ishbosheth was 40 years of age when he was placed on the throne by Abner (2 Sa. ii. 10), and this fact suggests a considerable reign for Saul.

xiii. 48. Extreme Calvinism has sought a foothold in this verse, but in so doing takes insufficient notice of context or language. Note: (i) The Jews had already 'judged themselves unworthy' (46). They had, in other words, exercised their will, and made their choice. Turning to the Gentiles, the apostles found faith among 'those who had ranged themselves for eternal life'. (ii) The verb, as the translation given immediately above suggests, is middle (middle and passive coincide in this tense) and thus implies some personal action. The metaphor is military. The 'Gentiles had set themselves in place', by faith, for eternal life. 'Ordained', of course, in the AV translation, is not necessarily indicative of a Calvinistic bias. In Jn. xv. 16 it translates 'placed'. See also Ps. viii. 3.

xiv. 1–3. The inconsequence which has been sometimes felt in these verses has led to numerous adjustments, including one ancient recasting of verse 2, and Moffatt's characteristic transposition of verses 2 and 3. The critical note by R. J. Knowling (*op. cit.*, II, p. 302) collects the evidence, and hazards a defence of the traditional order and text. Knowling writes, '. . . as the text stands it is quite possible to suppose that the effect of the preaching in the synagogue would be twofold, verse 2 thus answering to the last clause of verse 1, and that the disciples continued to speak boldly, encouraged by success on the one hand, and undeterred by opposition on the other, the consequence being that the division of the city was further intensified.'

xiv. 11. It is evident that the missionaries did not understand what the Lycaonians were saying in their native speech (a dialect akin to Gallic, according to St. Jerome, as one might expect in Galatia), and that they realized that blasphemy was afoot only when they discovered that sacrifice was being prepared in their honour. In bilingual Asia Minor, the people at large had understood the visitors' Greek. The mysterious 'gift of tongues' was evidently not a miraculous proficiency in unknown languages.

VIII. THE JERUSALEM CONFERENCE
(xiv. 27–xv. 35)

a. Report at Antioch (xiv. 27–xv. 3)

The Church was now established in the Gentile world, and those who had daringly commissioned Paul and Barnabas had important decisions to make. The older converts of Antioch had entered the Church by way of the synagogue, and had automatically accepted certain prohibitions as a rule of life. They had no thought of any other possibility. Two new factors, however, were fast becoming evident. First, Paul's view of the Law must have become the subject of widening and vigorous debate. Second, the new converts of Galatia knew nothing of Judaism and there is no evidence at all that Paul enforced upon them any preliminary condition of conformity to Jewish rules.

It is not possible here to go fully into the difficult question of harmonizing the accounts of subsequent events found in Galatians ii and Acts xv. Suffice it to observe that the admit-

tedly close association of the two authors presupposes agreement, especially in a matter so vital to the theme of both. It is
possible to claim that no discrepancy does, in fact, arise,
provided the chronological sequence of Gal. ii. 1–14 is not
unjustifiably pressed. The following paragraphs take that line.

A time-lapse is suggested by xiv. 28 during which the
problem was actively discussed and Paul's liberal solution
generally accepted. The situation envisaged in Galatians ii is
a harmonious one, with Christians of Jewish and non-Jewish
origin enjoying an unembarrassed fellowship which shocked a
deputation from Jerusalem. Luke does not identify these
emissaries. With marked reserve he speaks of them as *certain
men which came down from Judæa* (xv. 1). If the view is taken
that Peter was in Antioch, and that the clash between Peter
and Paul was prior to the Jerusalem Conference, the visitors
must have been sent expressly by James (Gal. ii. 12). The
Bezan text of verse 1 adds that they were Pharisees, a likely
surmise. The line taken by the Jerusalem visitors was a fairly
subtle one. They could hardly argue that one Christian should
not associate with another, but declared that no one could
become in a full sense a member of the Church unless he came
under the Law, and accepted the sign of the Law in his body.
All admitted that non-Jews could be accepted of God, but
was there a path of faith which did not follow the path of
history, through the ancient Law? Had God set aside the Law
of Moses? With Paul as a protagonist the vigour of the ensuing
debate can be imagined. 'Only rare and exceptional natures',
writes Ramsay,[1] 'could have risen unaided above the pride
and the prejudice of generations, and have sacrificed their law
to their advancing experience. The record confirms what we
see to be natural in the circumstances. Paul stood immovably
firm, and he carried with him, after some wavering the leaders
(but not the mass) of the Jewish Christians.'

The grace, consecration, and statesmanship of Paul, no less
than the determined and dynamic nature of his leadership,
must here be observed. Paul was a Hellenistic Jew, a Roman

[1] *St. Paul the Traveller and Roman Citizen* p. 157.

of Tarsus, and it must have been a temptation to his clear and ardent mind, accustomed to drive straight to a conclusion, to repudiate Jerusalem, and establish Gentile Christianity in a sphere free from the power, influence, and bigotry of the Pharisaism which he had himself so triumphantly rejected. But as an organizer and a statesman Paul saw that the Church must, in the meantime, have an administrative centre, and it is the measure of his greatness and magnanimity that he always recognized Jerusalem as fulfilling this function.

The visitors from Jerusalem seem to have brought matters to a crisis by their influence on Peter (Gal. ii. 12–14), and the sharp dissension which thereby arose between Peter and Paul. When Barnabas, in spite of the Galatian mission, was also carried away (Gal. ii. 13), the entire position of Gentile Christianity, and Paul's whole, hard-wrought conception of the gospel was forthwith under attack. Paul's appeal seems, judging from their later testimony (xv. 7–12), to have won back the two waverers, but it remained to convince the Jerusalem leaders, clearly a rigid group. An embassy was decided upon and despatched with some ceremony (3). Paul and Barnabas (and note Luke's order of the names, which is reversed in the Jerusalem context of verse 12) evidently went forth with the weight of the church of Antioch behind them. Verse 3 shows that they also accumulated support on the way.

b. Discussion at Jerusalem (xv. 4–29)

There was first a general meeting of the Christian community in Jerusalem to welcome the visitors and to hear their report (4). There followed a meeting of the apostolate and elders' court to deal with the controversial issues which the Pharisees seem to have tactlessly aired in the general assembly (5, 6). Here Peter, bravely and uncompromisingly, took his stand. His speech is singularly appropriate to his character, recalls the language of chapter x,[1] and conforms thoroughly to Paul's view. It is significant that upon this note Peter disappears

[1] R. B. Rackham, (*op. cit.*, footnotes, pp. 247, 248) analyses the language in detail.

from the story. Finally Paul, supported by Barnabas, stated the liberal position.

The debate is not summarized in detail. 'They of the circumcision' (xi. 2; Gal. ii. 12) were clearly a minority who were badly defeated in the logic of the argument. There seems, however, to have been a strong feeling that Jewish prejudice should not be roughly flouted. To render possible a real unanimity, the Gentiles, it was felt, should accept fundamental rules, the breaking of which seemed horrible to the Jews. So we gather from the able summary of the discussion by the chairman, James (13–21). All this was set forth in a formal decree (23–29), which was, in effect, a compromise. The extremists were disowned and condemned as 'subverting the soul' of the Gentiles. On the other hand, part of the Law is defined as 'quite necessary' (a most emphatic word is used in verse 28).

c. The application of the decree (xv. 30, 31)

There was a certain weakness in the compromise. The Pauline sympathizers would regard the imposition of certain legalities as a strong recommendation; the Judaizers would regard them as conditions of salvation. Thus there was forthwith a risk of two sects in the Church. In spite of the fact that Luke now dismisses the subject, the Epistles are indication enough that the controversy was not settled by the disowning of the extremists. In 1 Cor. viii. 4 Paul himself publicly adopts a more liberal attitude than that which the decree lays down. We know from the first Epistle to the Corinthians that, in spite of the efforts of the apostles, sects tended to emerge in the early Church. The danger, however, was mitigated by Christian familiarity with pagan practice. The 'mystery religions', Mithraism for example, had grades of initiates, and it may not have seemed unnatural to Gentile Christians to find a formal distinction between 'weaker' and 'stronger' brethren.

It was the grim march of history which broke the power of the Jerusalem—indeed, of the Palestinian—church and finally brushed aside the peril of a Judaistic interpretation of the gospel. The church in Jerusalem, it seems clear, became increasingly narrow. Paul felt himself to be under its condemnation (Acts xxi. 20-26; Rom. xv. 31), and, but for the vast disaster which fell on Palestine, the strong influence which proceeded from it might have been even more of a problem than it proved to be. At the insurrection of AD 66 the Christians of Jerusalem fled to Pella, and when Jerusalem lay desolate after its siege and destruction in AD 70, their influence was broken. In AD 132 occurred the last Jewish revolt, and when it was finally suppressed Hadrian founded the city of Aelia Capitolina on the site of Jerusalem, and all circumcised Jews were forbidden entry there, in grim contradiction of the oracle (Is. lii. 1) on which the opponents of Paul's gospel had based part of their case. Christians were admitted, if they gave up Judaism. One Marcus became the first bishop of Aelia, and Marcus was a Gentile. By such sombre processes was Jerusalem purged of its Judaistic Christians. Broken and ineffective, the old error nevertheless lived on. We hear of a sect called the Nazarenes in Syria as late as the fourth century; and the Ebionite heresy, which endured until the fourth century also, was based upon a Jewish adulteration of Christianity and a repudiation of Paul.

d. The unfolding plan (xv. 32-35)

With a picture of harmonious effort for the gospel's sake Luke draws near the end of a chapter which he has designed as a keystone in the arch of his book. The first half of the book showed the unfolding of a divine purpose to give the gospel of Christ to the Gentile world. The great issue is Judaism and the right of Christianity to an independent existence. Chapter xv shows the issue joined and settled officially in principle. In less than seven hundred words, 'in so masterly a way as to give the entire chapter the stamp of genius',[1] Luke has described a great turning-point in the history of Christianity and the world. Paul has triumphed. Much contention and disappointment await, as the letters of Paul abundantly show, but the eye

[1] F. J. Foakes-Jackson, *op. cit.*, p. 130.

of the historian rightly sees the finality of the events described in chapter xv. There victory began.

Now, in preparation for the next section of his narrative he sets forth the situation briefly. Antioch has become a strong base for the Pauline conception of the gospel. There were *many others also* (35), besides the two veterans, qualified 'to teach and preach the message of the Lord'. Such functions were vitally important before the consolidation and dissemination of the New Testament. Paul and Barnabas are now the recognized leaders of Gentile Christianity, their prestige increased since their visit to Jerusalem. Paul was to increase, as Barnabas passed to separate and unrecorded labours. Silas, a 'prophet also' (32), appears on the scene. Note Luke's method. Just as xii. 25 prepares the way for xiii. 5 so here xv. 34 prepares the way for xv. 40. It may have been at Paul's suggestion that Silas remained at Antioch when the joint embassy was completed. He had many notable qualifications for such partnership. He had the commendation and confidence of the Jerusalem church which Paul was anxious not to antagonize. He was also a Roman citizen, and emerges appropriately at the beginning of a movement in the story which is to end in Rome. Silvanus was his Latin name (1 Thes. i. 1), Silas being a familiar abbreviation. So the stage was set.

Additional Notes

xv. 1, 2. The tense is imperfect. The visitors 'set about teaching', with, it appears, some determination. Luke uses a strong word for the *dissension* (2) occasioned by this campaign. It is *stasis*, a word sadly frequent in the historical records of Greece. It is that discord and irreconcilable division, that factious opposition of parties in the state, of which many a Greek state died, which ruined Athenian democracy, and ripened Greece for the dictatorship of Macedon. The Greek church was running true to form, thanks to Jewish interference, when the strength and devotion of Paul, and the sincerity of Peter, saved the situation.

xv. 3. The delegation were *brought on their way*. The word occurs again at xx. 38, xxi. 5, xxviii. 15.

xv. 10. Moffatt adjusts the Greek text by the omission of the words for 'God'. The resultant meaning is, no doubt, smooth and consistent with the narrative ('Why are you trying to impose a yoke on the neck of the disciples'). Thus to tamper with the text in order to make the writer say what the translator would prefer him to have said, is a fault with which Moffatt may sometimes be charged. The only authority for the reading chosen is one Latin MS, and a few Latin patristic contexts. There is therefore no likelihood that Luke wrote what Moffatt renders. Bold emendation is justified only where no meaning can otherwise be extracted from the text. The words *tempt God* have, moreover, a clear enough meaning in Scripture. They mean to 'distrust His guidance, and in consequence disobey His revealed will'.[1] Cf. Ps. xcv. 9–11; 1 Cor. x. 9; Heb. iii. 9. Ananias and Sapphira are said to have 'agreed to tempt the Spirit of the Lord' by acting as though they thought they could deceive God (Acts v. 9).

xv. 12. The tenses again are interesting. The verse might be rendered: 'Then all the gathering fell silent, and they set themselves to hear Barnabas and Paul. . . .'

xv. 17. James quotes Amos from the Septuagint, which suggests that the proceedings, involving, as they did, Gentile Christians, were conducted in the Greek language. If Amos ix. 11, 12 is compared, it will be seen that the Septuagint differs considerably here from the traditional Hebrew text. Amos pictures the restored tabernacle, and the people of David, restored along with it, as the possessors of the remnant of Edom and all the heathen. The Septuagint, remarks Lumby,[2] 'as an exposition, speaks of "the residue of men seeking unto the restored tabernacle". St. James makes both clear by showing that "to seek after the Lord" is to be the true up-building both of the house of David and of all mankind besides.' It is

[1] J. R. Lumby, *op. cit.*, p. 274.
[2] *Op. cit.*, p. 277.

also worth remembering that the Hebrew for 'man' is *adam*, whose consonants are identical with those of 'Edom'. 'Remnant of Edom' and *residue of men* are therefore identical in an unpointed text.[1] The Dead Sea Scrolls have already taught us that the Septuagint is a translation to be respected for its retention of a sound textual tradition.

xv. 24. The verb translated *subverting*, which occurs only here, is used in Classical Greek for the entire removal of a person's furniture and possessions. The effect of the Judaistic heresy was, it suggests, to turn the mental furniture of the Gentile converts upside down, and to destroy the ordered comfort of their minds.

xv. 31, 32. The AV translates *paraklēsis* of 31 by *consolation*, but renders the cognate verb (*parekalesan*) of 32 by *exhorted*. 'Consoled' is the correct translation, and the word is eloquent of the comfort the letter from Jerusalem brought. The Gentile Christians clearly accepted the communication as a gracious compromise, and a magnanimous attempt to meet their wishes.

IX. INTO EUROPE (xv. 36–xvii. 14)

a. Antioch again (xv. 36–39)

Paul remained in the central city of Gentile Christianity until the differences with Jerusalem were resolved in the compromise arrangements recorded in chapter xv. He then felt moved to traverse again the old Asian preaching-ground and confirm the converts. His assumption of leadership is to be noted (36).

Luke now conscientiously records a sad *contention* (39) between the two partners. The word used is a strong one (*paroxusmos*), and the AV rendering is correct in adding the adjective *sharp*. Paul and Barnabas *departed asunder*, and in the Greek an uncommonly strong expression is again employed. In the New Testament the verb occurs again only at Rev. vi.

[1] See F. F. Bruce, *op. cit.*, p. 298.

14, where the heavens 'departed' in apocalyptic disaster. Paul was a vehement character, inclined to strong reactions (xxiii. 3), and particularly sensitive to what he considered disloyalty or laggard response to his leadership (Phil. ii. 20, 21). Love, he writes in 1 Cor. xiii. 5, perhaps a little self-reproachfully, 'is not easily provoked', and he actually uses the verb cognate with the noun *paroxusmos*. A few years later, it is pleasant to note, Barnabas is the subject of a friendly word (Col. iv. 10; 2 Tim. iv. 11). In a sense the perilous division turned out for good. Cyprus, Barnabas' native isle, was visited again, and the competent Silas enlisted in the work.

b. Syria and Cilicia (xv. 40, 41)

Setting out from Antioch, Paul and Silas traversed the gorge of the Amanus and the 'Syrian Gates', and entered Cilicia. The region had been slow in submitting to the Greek influence which was so potent in Asia Minor and the Middle East. Phoenician influence had been strong, and had left a tradition of seamanship. The coastal areas, in fact, were the haunt of the great pirate fleets which, a century before, had terrorized the Mediterranean. Such lawlessness was long since tamed under the strong administration of Rome, but the area remained a backwater, heavily infected, as its coinage shows, by Oriental paganism, and not the type of territory where Paul exercised his most characteristic ministry. It was, of course, his home province, and a man of Tarsus could hardly pass by the remoter countryside of his own homeland. Luke, who is not yet writing as a member of the party, could hardly be more brief in describing a mission of perhaps some weeks or months (41). It would appear that Paul, who no doubt supplied the details, looked upon the campaign as a routine task, not a major movement in the evangelization of Anatolia, and without notable or significant incidents.

c. Galatia again (xvi. 1-5)

The region of earlier evangelization was beckoning, and Paul and Silas left the coastal plain and made for the high country

by the only route which crossed the Taurus Range, the famous
'Cilician Gates', through which Alexander had marched to
conquer the vast Persian Empire, four centuries before.
The narrative still appears to hurry, either because Paul did
not regard this second visit as worthy of detailed report, or
because Luke himself chooses to hasten on to the momentous
events of the European ministry and the visit to Philippi. One
event, however, delays the narrative, the call of Timothy, who
takes up the youthful ministry relinquished by John Mark.

Derbe and Lystra (1) were a single administrative 'region',
and the latter town appears to have been Timothy's birthplace
(2). Geographically Lystra is linked with Iconium (2), in spite
of the administrative grouping, and Paul appears to have taken
note of Timothy's reputation in the whole district. The preoccupation with character in those who assume Christian
leadership is a marked feature of the story of the early Church
(vi. 3, x. 22, xxii. 12). The visit to Lystra and Derbe was a
private affair. 'He' of verse 1 becomes 'they' of verse 4.

Verses 3 and 4 raise a difficult question. Why did Paul
circumcise the young Hellenistic Jew? The action is certainly
indicative of his concern, at this stage, not in any way to offend
the susceptibilities of the Jews, whose colonies were grouped
along the intended route through Pisidian Antioch and
Iconium. The rite, Bruce suggests,[1] may have been to 'legiti-
matize' Timothy in Jewish eyes. Otherwise he would rank as
a Gentile. Why even this should matter is a question without
obvious answer consistent with Paul's position.

At any rate, Luke sees fit to mention in juxtaposition the
circumcision of Timothy, and the faithful publication of the
Jerusalem decree. Why are these details stressed? No doubt
because of the later situation in Galatia, known to Luke at the
time of writing, where Jewish action was such that Paul felt
absolved from any further obligation to publish or enforce the
decisions of the Jerusalem elders. Certain it is that the advice
to the Corinthians on 'meat offered to idols' strains the decree
to the utmost.

[1] *Op. cit.*, p. 308.

It appears that, hard on Paul's heels, came missionaries of the Judaizing party. Their action must have made him bitterly regret the second mile of well-meaning compromise he had gone in the matter of Timothy. Picking on his action, they claimed that he 'preached circumcision' (Gal. v. 11). Paul, Rackham points out,[1] enters so fully into the question of Titus' circumcision (Gal. i. 10, ii. 3–5, v. 11) because he is at the same time defending his action with Timothy. He must, none the less, have bitterly regretted such a need for defence, and Ramsay's comment[2] may not be unjust: 'No act of Paul's whole life', he writes, 'is more difficult to sympathize with; none cost him dearer. . . .'

It is easier to be wise after the event, and the future history of Galatia belongs rather to the exposition of the vehement Epistle to the Galatians than to Luke's account of the second missionary journey. Let it suffice to point out in conclusion how vital the area was to Paul's whole ministry. 'If these churches,' writes Ramsay,[3] 'his first foundations towards the west, were to pass under the party of slavery, his work was ruined at its inception; the blow to his policy and influence was ruinous.' How near such disaster came, the situation visible some little time later was to show. Paul, at least, had done his utmost to conserve his work. He had acted honourably and faithfully. If he also acted unwisely in the matter of Timothy, the unwisdom sprang from a generous heart, and a willingness to conciliate and please which found scant response in those who became his enemies.

d. Asia (xvi. 6–8)

'It is quite evident', writes Rackham,[4] 'that the paragraph xvi. 6–10 begins a new division in the Acts.' This is very true. Paul's party traversed 'the Phrygian region of Galatia'. Note this rendering of the phrase which the AV gives as *Phrygia and the region of Galatia*. Literally translated the Greek text says:

[1] *Op. cit.*, p. 263.
[2] *Pauline Studies*, p. 35.
[3] *St. Paul the Traveller and Roman Citizen*, p. 184.
[4] *Op. cit.*, p. 271.

'the Phrygian and the Galatian region', and this can only mean that area of the province which was both Phrygian and Galatian. At this point geography becomes important. Phrygia was an ancient part of Asia Minor noted in legend and history. It was rich, for it straddled old trade routes which ran into continental Asia, and its civilization was early and precocious, as archaeology shows. In Roman times the area was comprehended in the provinces of Asia and Galatia. Of the latter province the northern portion was wild and uncivilized, and populated largely by the Gallo-Celtic tribesmen who had broken into Asia Minor in an old tribal migration, and had given Galatia its name. The southern portion was sophisticated and civilized, and included such cities as Antioch and Iconium. Some have contended that Paul's Galatian churches, those to whom he addressed his letter, were in the north. It was argued that the southern area was Greek not Phrygian, that the instability of the Galatian churches under the impact of Judaism was a reaction of Celtic headiness, and so forth. Ramsay's careful collection of epigraphical evidence has, however, satisfactorily proved that the recipients of the letter were the South Galatian churches, and that Luke's geographical terminology was precise. One inscription speaks of the 'Phrygian' Antioch, and others have made it obvious that the administrative district of South Galatia was Phrygian in language and tradition. There was, moreover, an uprooted minority of Jews whose presence accounts for the Judaistic tendencies of the Church. It is clear, too, on epigraphical as well as historical evidence, that the area was evangelized in early days. It offers a very large corpus of Christian inscriptions, which, incidentally, testify to the high standard of literacy of the Asian Christians. The demonstration that the Galatia of the New Testament was South Galatia made the theory of those critics who regarded the Acts of the Apostles as a late, apologetic fabrication no longer tenable. It stands proven that the Galatian passages could only have been written by a first-century historian who wrote naturally in the geographical terminology of contemporary inscriptions.

Having traversed this region the party crossed into the Roman province of Asia, but found themselves prevented from preaching there. Whatever form the hindrance took, Paul regarded it as divine guidance. They passed into Mysia, and swung north to Bithynia, but another of those compulsions which Paul took to be God's guidance constrained them to turn west to Alexandria Troas. (It is interesting to note that these regions where Paul was forbidden to preach were not passed by in the progress of the gospel. There is evidence of very early foundations in Mysia, and for Bithynia there is the evidence of Pliny's famous letters. This Roman governor, writing sixty years later, speaks of the grip which Christianity had secured over his province, and the measures of repression undertaken by him.)

e. Troas (xvi. 9–11)

Paul would have felt at home here. Troas was a Roman colony, whose proximity to ancient Troy, from which Rome claimed descent, had secured privileges from the imperial administration. And yet he must have been in a strangely disturbed state of mind. To Troas Paul had been driven by a strong compulsion almost against his judgment and will. The 'sweep and rush of the narrative', to use Ramsay's phrase, is unique. The natural development of Paul's work along the great central highway of the Empire was first *forbidden* (6). The obvious alternative was likewise overruled, *the Spirit suffered them not* (7). He had been led across Asia from the south-east to the north-west corner, and had yet been prevented from preaching in its borders. Everything must have been dark and perplexing until, in a flash of revelation, the vision at Troas made all things plain (9).

It has been plausibly suggested, first by Renan, and then by Sir William Ramsay, who later abandoned the theory, that the *man of Macedonia* who figured in the dream was Luke himself. 'They' in the narrative becomes 'we' at verse 10, indicating that Luke first joined the company before Paul crossed into Europe. Luke was a physician and Philippi was a seat of medical science. It is not wholly unlikely that Luke, hearing of miracles of healing, journeyed to Asia Minor under the same compulsion which had brought Paul to its western borders. An interview with Paul followed. In his sleep that night Paul, in the disturbed dreaming which often follows indecision, saw 'a certain man from Macedonia' (9). The Greek pronoun suggests that he could name him if he would. The Macedonians had no distinctive dress. The Turk divided Asia from Europe at the Dardanelles. To cross that famous strait in the ancient world was not a passage from East to West, and involved no great consciousness of change. It was the Adriatic Sea which divided the Greek and Roman world. The Aegean and the Hellespont merely flowed between two Greek-speaking provinces of the Empire. How did Paul recognize the visitant of his dream as a man from Macedonia, if he did not know him as an individual?

Other details in the narrative also suggest that Luke was a Philippian. In verse 12, for example, Luke describes Philippi as 'a city of Macedonia, the first of the district, a Roman colony' (RV). Amphipolis was, in fact, the capital. As a touch of enthusiasm and loyalty to a home town, the expression is quite understandable. Nor is there distortion of fact. 'After-wards', writes Ramsay,[1] 'Philippi quite outstripped its rival; but it was at that time in such a position that Amphipolis was ranked first by general consent, Philippi first by its own consent. These cases of rivalry between two or even three cities for the dignity and title of "first" are familiar to every student of the history of the Greek cities; and though no other evidence is known to show that Philippi had as yet begun to claim the title, yet this single passage is conclusive. The descriptive phrase is like a lightning-flash in the darkness of local history, revealing in startling clearness the whole situation to those whose eyes were trained to catch the character of Greek city history. . . .' It is odd to see the personality of the historian peep out. And how is one to explain the touch of warmth unless Luke was a Philippian? Rackham's very fair

[1] *St. Paul the Traveller and Roman Citizen*, pp. 206, 207.

criticism of this view is found on pp. 278, 280, 281 of his commentary.

f. Philippi (xvi. 12)

It adds some force to the suggestion that Luke was a Philippian when the route from Asia Minor to Europe is traced on the map. The party spent a night in Samothrace, landed at Neapolis, and proceeded straight to Philippi by the Via Egnatia, the Roman arterial road which connected Dyrrachium with the Aegean Coast.

The scheme fell in with Paul's conception of evangelism. His vision of a victorious gospel embraced the Roman world. He saw the great totalitarian state knit into a mighty whole from Palestine to Spain by the authority of the Emperor and that reverence for him which was later to be exalted into a religion. He saw the strong-points, the strategic bases, held by the legions. He saw the network of roads which ensured their mobility, and which passed as arteries of trade, culture, and defence through all the wide provinces from the Thames to the Nile. It fascinated him, and the conscious object of his life was the capture of those strategic bases for Christ. His projected visit to Spain (Rom. xv. 24, 28), and his eagerness to reach Rome itself, are related to this preoccupation.

Philippi was pre-eminently a base of Empire. Philip, father of Alexander the Great, founded the town, or at least re-fortified it, in 356 BC, and that old villain's eye for a strategic position dominating the cross-roads of northern Greece wanted nothing in acuteness. It is not without similar significance that the Battle of Philippi, in the strife which followed the assassination of Julius Caesar, was fought at this point a century before Paul's visit. Like Belgium and Palestine, the plain was a cockpit of history. For the same reason the Emperor Augustus, finally victorious over his foes, founded a colony for his demobilized veterans at Philippi. The gaoler might have been a grandson of one of these legionaries. There was also a school of medicine in the town, connected with one of those guilds of doctors which the followers of early Greek medicine had

scattered up and down the world. It was a typical strong-point
of the Roman Empire, lying astride a great trade route. To
found a church there was a triumph of evangelism.

g. The gospel in Europe (xvi. 13-40)

The Jews had some meeting-place *by a river side* (13). Just as
we say 'to town' for a goal which the person addressed knows
familiarly and well, so Greek omits the definite article when
the place concerned is one within the close experience of the
speaker. Luke omits the article in the phrase quoted from
verse 13. It is another indication that he knew Philippi well.
Jewish communities preferred to meet for prayer by the sea or
a river, in places where they were too few in number or too
poor to possess a synagogue. Psalm cxxxvii gives a touching
picture of such a meeting, under the eyes of a curious crowd, by
the willow-lined Euphrates.

If Luke is the first Philippian we meet, Lydia is the second.
This 'seller of purple' came from Thyatira in Asia Minor.
Archaeology has shown that place to be a centre of varied
trade, and Lydia represented some firm engaged in marketing
cloth dyed 'turkey-red', from the juice of the madder-root.
The dye was a cheaper rival for the crimson expensively
extracted from the murex shell. Lydia became a Jewish
proselyte, through the influence, no doubt, of the Jewish
synagogue in her home town. Ramsay is of the opinion that it
was a corrupt organization which sponsored a hybrid worship,
half-Jewish, half-pagan. Hence the influence in later years of
'that woman Jezebel' (Rev. ii. 20), who sought to lead the
infant church astray.[1]

The slave-girl (16), in Ramsay's opinion, was a ventriloquist
whose mind had been turned by her strange gift. In the grip
of Satanic influence she was a source of profit to her un-
scrupulous owners. Like many such, she recognized goodness
when it crossed her path, and the human part of her responded
and called for help. Her cure destroyed the perilous gift which

---

[1] *The Letters to the Seven Churches*, pp. 327-353; or, more accessibly, *The
Seven Churches* (E. M. Blaiklock), pp. 41-51.

made her valuable, and Philippi saw what Ephesus saw later, a source of pagan gain stopped by the victorious gospel.

Hence arrest and a tumultuous trial (22). Paul obviously was given no opportunity to mention the fact of his Roman citizenship, which sobered the excited officials so effectively the next morning (38). The proceedings were most disorderly and irregular. (In a speech for the prosecution against Verres, the tyrant governor of Sicily, Cicero speaks with horror of a Roman citizen who was scourged while protesting 'in the midst of his pain and the noise of the blows, "I am a Roman citizen".'[1] It was regarded as a most serious offence to make such a claim untruthfully, or to disregard it if truthfully made.)

Ramsay writes of the night in prison: 'Anyone who has seen a Turkish prison will not wonder that the doors were thrown open; each door was merely closed by a bar, and the earthquake as it passed along the ground forced the doorposts apart, so that the bar slipped from its hold, and the door swung open. The prisoners were fastened to the wall or in wooden stocks (24); the chains and stocks were detached from the wall which was shaken so that spaces gaped between the stones. In the great earthquakes of 1880 at Smyrna, and 1881 at Scio, I had the opportunity of seeing and hearing of the strangely capricious action of an earthquake which behaves sometimes like a playful sprite, when it spares its full terrors.'[2] Such was the natural machinery. Why did not the prisoners escape? Ramsay speaks of the northern 'self-centred tenacity of purpose and presence of mind' absent in an excitable Oriental people. This, and fear of the gaoler, accounts for the rank and file. Paul and Silas had a policy, expressed in verse 37. They were unafraid (25, 28), and determined both to abide God's will, and to secure justice.

The gaoler is rapidly sketched. His stern devotion to duty (27) is apparent; so, too, are his rapid recognition of Paul's spiritual leadership (30), his clear-cut decision (33), his kindly, practical response (33), his evident leadership in his own household (34). (Verse 34 explains verse 31. No 'household

[1] *In Verr.* v. 62. [2] *St. Paul the Traveller and Roman Citizen*, pp. 220, 221.

salvation' on the strength of the faith of the head of the house is implied. All believed.)

The marks of first-hand authentic narrative are obvious. Note the gruff attempt of the now frightened magistrates to preserve their dignity and get rid of their embarrassing prisoners (35); note how the gaoler's rendering softens the words (36). Paul 'calls their bluff' (37). They had no right to flog a Roman, even condemned. The word *uncondemned* (cf. xxii. 25) is probably Luke's free rendering of the Latin *re incognita*, 'with the case unheard'. Paul's point would be that only a plea of ignorance could excuse flogging a Roman, but that such a plea at least presupposed a trial. (Ramsay's suggestion[1] that Paul first claimed Roman privilege in Philippi because he was just beginning, at this point in his career, to realize 'the relationship of the Church to the Empire', is not a likely solution of the difficulty. The influence of Silas is not impossible.)

h. Thessalonica (xvii. 1–9)

Leaving Philippi, Paul and Silas followed the Via Egnatia in the direction of Amphipolis, a short distance from the mouth of the Strymon. Passing through both Amphipolis and Apollonia, they reached Thessalonica at the head of its gulf. It was a prosperous sea-port, as its prolific coinage shows.

Paul's ministry began with a composite group, the Jews of the synagogue, some Greek proselytes and, included among these, a number of ladies of standing. In Macedonia, as in parts of Asia Minor, women were more emancipated than they were in some portions of the Greek world. The theme of the apostle's ministry is summarized in verse 3.

Trouble arose from the now familiar source (1 Thes. ii. 14–16). The description of the riot reinforces the impression made by an analysis of Paul's audience that, contrary to Gibbon's once accepted opinion, the gospel found its first and widest acceptance among the educated.[2] The lower classes,

---

[1] *Luke the Physician*, p. 25.
[2] Ramsay, *The Church in the Roman Empire*, p. 57.

the least educated elements, formed the superstitious raw material of the Jews' rabble-rousing. The *lewd fellows of the baser sort* (5) are literally, 'bad men from among the market people', the labourers, no doubt, and humbler trade-associates of the Jewish commercial houses. Mt. xx. 3 pictures those who stood 'idle in the market-place' awaiting work. The desperate have often become the tools and dupes of the evil. So they were at Thessalonica.

Roman law depended on voluntary prosecutors to set its processes in motion. Hence the approach to the *rulers* (8). Luke twice (6 and 8) calls these officials 'politarchs'. Since the term was unknown elsewhere, the critics of Luke once dismissed it as a mark of ignorance. Sixteen epigraphical examples now exist in modern Salonica, and one is located in the British Museum on a stone which once formed part of an archway. It was evidently a Macedonian term. It was Luke's general practice to use the term in commonest use in educated circles. Hence he called the officials of Philippi 'praetors', and an inscription has similarly established the fact that this was a courtesy title given to the magistrates of a Roman colony.

The charge was subtly conceived and dangerous. The mention of treason compelled the politarchs to act, and under the circumstances their binding over of the accused on Jason's bond of security was a mild action. It was none the less effective. It seems to imply a guarantee from Jason that Paul would go and not return. Hence 1 Thes. ii. 18. From 1 Thes. ii. 13, 14, iii. 3, it appears that local persecution continued. Still the church became a centre of evangelism, and included elements of the first audience (1 Thes. i. 8, 9). The first two chapters of the first letter to Thessalonica imply a stay of some length, in spite of the brevity of Luke's account. Ramsay suggests December, 50 to May, 51.

i. Berea (xvii. 10-14)

So far events in Europe had given Paul no reason to hope that it would be easier to preach the gospel west of the Hellespont. The old troubles of Asia had followed him across. Berea was at first a happier experience. Among the Jews, *more noble than those in Thessalonica* (11), there was at first a notable freedom from the endemic jealousy of their race. Understanding the word 'noble' in a social sense, Rackham[1] argues that the Berean Jews were more open to conviction because of an aristocratic background, and presumably a better education. This is not impossible, and the word is twice used in the New Testament in this sense (Lk. xix. 12; 1 Cor. i. 26). Luke, however, does define his meaning, and it seems clear from the explanatory clause that he calls the Bereans 'more noble' because their conduct contrasted with that of the Thessalonian mob and those who descended to their base level. These agitators soon arrived in the town, and the process of slander and persecution was evidently repeated. The lightness with which Luke passes over the dangers which drove Paul from place to place probably reflects the nonchalance of the informant.

Verses 14 and 15 require a little unravelling. F. F. Bruce[2] reconstructs events thus. (i) Paul leaves Silas and Timothy in Berea, and goes to Athens, whence he sends them a message to rejoin him at once (14, 15). It should be remembered that Paul left Berea with no fixed plan, and was anxious to return to Thessalonica (1 Thes. ii. 17, 18). Silas and Timothy were evidently left behind to await news of the attitude of the new city magistrates. In Athens, Paul saw more clearly the development of his plan, and drew his team together again. (ii) They rejoin him at Athens (cf. 1 Thes. iii. 1). (iii) Paul sends Timothy to Thessalonica (1 Thes. iii. 1, 2), and Silas to some other part of Macedonia (Acts xviii. 5). Ramsay suggests he went to Philippi. (iv) Paul goes on to Corinth (Acts xviii. 1). (v) Silas and Timothy return from Macedonia to Corinth (Acts xviii. 5; 1 Thes. iii. 6). (vi) From Corinth Paul writes both letters to the Thessalonians.

Additional Notes

xv. 39. The word *paroxusmos* occurs twice in the Septuagint: at Dt. xxix. 28, where it is the second of the three words used

---

[1] *Op. cit.*, p. 299.   [2] *Op. cit.*, pp. 329, 330.

for the severity of God, and at Je. xxxii. 37 which refers to the earlier passage.

xvi. 13. It is possible that there was a building by the riverside. The clause rendered in AV *where prayer was wont to be made* could mean 'where a place of prayer was thought to be', or, following another well-supported reading, 'where we thought there was a place of prayer'. The word *proseuchē* can mean both 'prayer' and 'place of prayer', and a Latin context shows that the second sense became widely known in the Gentile world. In Juvenal's picture of the inconveniences of Rome (*Sat.* iii. 295) the bully who accosts the benighted traveller bawls: '*ede ubi consistas, in qua te quaero proseucha?*', 'out with it where's your stand, in what bethel am I to find you?' On the whole, in the light of practice documented from Psalm cxxxvii to Tertullian, the traditional rendering is to be preferred.

xvi. 14. The following more clearly gives the sense: 'And a woman named Lydia, a seller of purple of the city of Thyatira and a worshipper of God, used to listen to them. And her heart the Lord opened so that she paid attention to Paul's words.'

xvii. 6. There is a colloquial tang about the language which fits well with the vulgar character of the force recruited for the riot. In a famous papyrus a spoilt urchin writes to his father, and threatens childish reprisals if he is not taken to Alexandria. Reporting his trials at home he quotes his mother's appeal to a servant or an elder brother: 'He upsets me, take him away.' The word for 'upset' is the one used in this verse for *turning the world upside down* (AV).

xvii. 9. Rackham[1] quotes an interesting papyrus letter (*O.P.* ii. 294, Grenfell and Hunt) concerning the 'security'. It is dated AD 22. In his absence from home, one Serapion's house had been searched, and he appeals to the prefect. Meanwhile two of the officials responsible were to be held in custody until the session of the prefectural court, 'unless they persuade the chief usher to give security for them. . . .'

[1] *Op. cit.*, p. 298.

X. ATHENS (xvii. 15-34)

The Athens of this vivid story was in the late afternoon of her glory. The great Greek city had once led the world in its intellectual achievement and the ardour of its spirit. That was five centuries before, in the fifty years of one of Europe's golden ages. There are times in the affairs of men when the spring-tide seems to pause at its flood, eras when, for a span of years, the minds of men are filled with ideas which they find completely satisfying, and poet, artist, and statesman find satisfaction and fulfilment in expressing in art and institution a stable and a tested faith. Athens knew such an epoch and saw its glory fade and pass. It is worth while to turn the records and ask why.

The great achievements of men are always the fruit of the spirit's response to a challenge, be it of danger, difficulty, or hardship. Like the Elizabethan era of England, the age of Pericles followed a triumphant struggle with a great peril from abroad. The beginning of the fifth century saw such an up-boiling of Asia as our own age has known. Hellas, whose greatest muster was something over one hundred thousand fighting men, broke in battle on sea and land the hosts of the Persian king, fed by the wealth and manpower of an empire which extended from the Dardanelles to the Indus, and from the Caspian to Assouan on the Nile. In the forefront of the fight stood Athens. Hers were the spearmen whose thin lines pushed the Persians into the sea at Marathon, hers the ships which bore the brunt of battle in the straits of Salamis, hers the land whose farms were burned and stripped by the invading host, and hers the city which, emptied of its citizens, found at Xerxes' hands destruction more complete than London or Berlin in Hitler's war.

The Athenian response to this mighty challenge was an outburst of spiritual energy scarce paralleled in history. In a mood of exaltation which believed all things possible to the conquerors of Persia, the people of Attica set to work. They equipped their farmlands with buildings which, three generations later, their Theban enemies found it worth while to dismantle and transfer bodily to Boeotia.[1] They rebuilt their shattered city and filled it with monuments, some of which have survived the incredible battering of twenty-three centuries and stand today, a monument to the worth of human effort when willing hands work as one under the inspiration of a grand idea. 'In this work', says a modern historian,[2] 'Periclean Athens displayed a vitality far superior to that of post-war France. When the French recovered the battered shell of Rheims Cathedral, they performed a pious restoration of each shattered stone and splintered statue. When the Athenians found the Hekatompedon burnt down to the foundations, they let the foundations lie, and proceeded, on a new site, to create the Parthenon.'

In a new-born passion for freedom, Athens founded a democracy, and gave expression to principles of liberty which still ring on the lips of men. Of the world's four supreme tragic artists, fifth-century Athens produced three. With Aeschylus, Sophocles, and Euripides stands only Shakespeare. The age produced Thucydides, finest, in Macaulay's judgment, of all historians. It produced the noblest European mind, Plato, at once the greatest thinker and greatest writer of the ancient world; and Socrates, who never wrote, but who lives in Plato's thought and work.

The fifth century produced some of mankind's noblest art, and that is asserted in spite of the archaists. Much of the revolt against Classical Greek art is the reaction of a dissatisfied and unhappy age against the serenity of a more stable society which believed it knew where perfection lay and expressed itself with confidence.

In language, itself an art, Athens produced what is perhaps the most perfect instrument of human expression in the history of speech. Words are the symbols of creative thought. Language reflects the quality of the minds which give it shape and form. If the spirit of Athens at her best was permeated with the

---

[1] *Hellen. Oxy.*, xii. 3–4.
[2] A. J. Toynbee, *The Study of History*, II, p. 110.

passion for truth, one should expect to find that mood translated into the forms of speech.[1] The amazingly subtle verb, the
rich facilities of the article, the brilliant invention of the
particle which Attic Greek carried to final perfection and
which enabled the written sentence without stage directions to
express irony, deprecate, cock an eyebrow, curl the lip, shrug
the shoulders, and represent, in short, to the reading eye the
animation of the living voice, these are only three of the many
qualities which made Attic speech perhaps the world's most
powerful and exact linguistic medium. For vivid conversation
and the expression of abstract thought this is most certainly
true.

These are a few of the achievements of Athens' Periclean
age. Dead for eighteen centuries, with their record perilously
preserved in a few hundred manuscripts, they availed by their
mere wonder to stir the thought of Europe to new life in the
days of the Renaissance.

Athens' glory in literature, art, and thought withered in a
generation. Its monuments remained in stone and written
speech. Personalities survived like people 'left on earth after a
judgment day'. Looking back we can see, nevertheless, that
the disastrous Twenty-Seven Years' war with Sparta was a
conflict in which 'one unhappy generation of Hellenes dealt
their own Hellas a mortal blow, and knew that her blood was
on them and their children'.[2] Those who watched thought of
Aeschylus and Herodotus, and remembered three Greek words
which were part of the century's contribution to historical
thought—*koros*, *hubris*, *atē*. With considerable loss of moral
content the words may be translated 'surfeit', 'arrogant
behaviour', and 'disaster'. The first suggests the demoraliza-
tion which comes with prosperity or too complete success, the

[1] Compare Davidson's remark about Hebrew: '. . . If he [the learner]
goes forward to the study of the language with a faith in its regularity he
will find its very phonetic and grammatical principles to be instinct with
something of that sweet reasonableness, that sense of fair play, we might
almost say that passion for justice for which the Old Testament in the
sphere of human life so persistently and eloquently pleads.' (*Hebrew Grammar*,
Introduction, p. 3.)
[2] Toynbee, *op. cit.*, III, p. 292.

relaxing of the moral fibre in the favoured of fortune; the second implies the consequent loss of mental and moral balance reflected in over-confidence and outrageous action. Jeshurun,[1] as the Hebrew parable puts it, waxes fat and kicks. The third word, also oddly Hebraic in force, contains the notion of the mad blind impulse, by which the spirit, morally ripe for disaster and in the grip of sin unpardonable, is driven into the catastrophic folly of attempting the impossible. However differently the thought of another age may view the relations of cause and effect, the formula covers Athens. That is why the spectacle contains the elements of Aristotelian tragedy and stirs salutary pity and fear.

The war with Sparta revealed the ravages of decay. It becomes obvious, as the record proceeds, that 'ichabod' is written and that Athens is in full career for the sorry days half a century later which felt the lash of Demosthenes' tongue. The war with Sparta seems to have burned something from Athens' life which never found strength again. The great days died with the fifth century, and the fourth saw the rise of Macedon and the blight of her northern dictatorship lying over the land. In cynical recognition of her ancient achievement, Macedon allowed Athens to retain a measure of her ancient freedom. So, two dull and fruitless centuries later, did Rome. When Rome took over Greece in 146 BC the Romans allowed the city to hold a portion of her liberty within the framework of the Roman system. Athens lived on her past, became a great university centre, and the inevitable finishing school for bilingual Roman aristocrats.

A portion of Athens' inspiration, to be sure, had been incorporated in international Hellenism, had gone east with Alexander, and was remembered and admired in the complex of lands where, after his conquests, Greek became a second language, the Greek spirit a mental stimulus, and cosmopolitan Greeks an element in the population. But over all these long years of historical development, the city lay dead as though exhausted by the outburst of her fifth-century creativity.

[1] Dt. xxxii. 15.

Nothing replaces a living soul. The vibrant life which made the glory of the fifth century, lingered into the fourth with Plato, and flickered briefly as Demosthenes fought looming dictatorship with his tongue, was dead, and a proud people lived incongruously on the memory of it. The third century had seen the rise of the systems of the Epicureans and the Stoics, both philosophies of breakdown and despair. The old questing spirit sickened into curiosity, and the search for truth into cynicism. Such was the city to which Paul of Tarsus came.

a. The visitor (xvii. 15-17)

Paul, following that policy of adaptation (1 Cor. ix. 22) which was part of his method, adopted in Athens the Socratic practice of free discussion in the market-place (17). 'The mere Jew', writes Ramsay,[1] 'could never have assumed the Attic tone as Paul did. He was the student of a great university, visiting an older but yet a kindred university, surveying it with appreciative admiration, and mixing in its society as an equal. . . .' 'The extraordinary versatility of Paul's character,' Ramsay continues, 'the unequalled freedom and ease with which he walked in every society, and addressed so many races within the Roman world, were evidently appreciated by the man who wrote this narrative, for the rest of chapter xvii is as different in tone from xiii as Athens is different from Phrygia. In Ephesus Paul taught "in the school of Tyrannus"; in the city of Socrates he discussed moral questions in the market-place. How incongruous it would seem if the methods were transposed. But the narrative never makes a false step amid all the many details, as the scene changes from city to city; and that is the conclusive proof that it is a picture of real life.'

While Paul waited in Athens for the word he expected from Thessalonica (16), he was 'strongly moved' by the vast array of Athens' symbols, shrines, and accoutrements of pagan worship, and found it impossible to keep silence. Looking with delight on the still magnificent ruins of the Parthenon, which

[1] *St. Paul the Traveller and Roman Citizen*, p. 238.

Paul saw in its mellow glory, a modern Christian feels no such sharp resentment, and even regrets the loss of Athena's mighty statue, whose gleaming spear-point was visible forty miles away. The fact, of course, is that the issues which so stirred the Jewish visitor are dead. His nation had fought a bitter battle with idolatry whose course can be traced through the whole prophetic literature of the Old Testament. That is why it was not the beauty and art piled on Athens' Acropolis which stirred him. The thought of crude religion there represented was too obtrusive. Nor must the surviving pieces of Greek art obscure the fact that, in the name of religion or superstition, sculptures far more offensive defaced the town, the 'herms', for example, roughly fashioned with phallic attributes, which stood as protecting talismans at every entrance in the city. The famous case of their mutilation on the eve of the ill-starred Sicilian expedition in 415 BC is indication that Athens regarded her minor images with most superstitious concern.

It was easy to talk in Athens, and a man with a burden on his soul soon found occasion to put his convictions into speech. The word speedily reached the intelligentsia. 'What would this seed-picker say?' they asked (18), using a word which occurs in Aristophanes for birds of the plough-land, hopping here and there in rapid selection of varied seed. It was Athenian slang for the philosophic picker-up of oddments, the visiting preacher with ideas incongruously mingled, and tags of thought and religion to expound. The great city was the goal of many such seekers after fortune. The courteous request addressed directly to Paul (19, 20) indicates that, in spite of the sophisticated slang of their private communications, the philosophers recognized something different in the visitor, and observed the decencies of social intercourse in issuing their invitation. Luke's touch of impatience in verse 21 is not, as some would have it, a piece of Macedonian sarcasm against an ancient enemy, but the simple truth. The curiosity of the Athenians was inveterate and age-old. Writing four and a half centuries before Luke, Thucydides (iii. 38) makes the demagogue Cleon complain that his people habitually play the part of 'spectators in displays of oratory and listeners to the tales of others' doings'. Half a century later Demosthenes (*Phil.* i. 43) contrasted their feckless curiosity with the vigour and drive of the dictator of Macedon. See also Theophrastus' *Characters*, iii. (4th century.)

b. The audience (xvii. 18-21)

The venerable court of the Areopagus retained its prestige under the Romans, and seems to have had some authority in religious matters. It may also have had the power to appoint public lecturers, and to exercise some control over them. Its members fell into two groups, as followers of the two great philosophic schools which divided the world (18).

The *Epicureans* (18) were the followers of the Athenian Epicurus, who lived from 341 to 270 BC. It was a weary age of breakdown and trouble, and Epicurus' philosophy of materialism and despair sprang naturally from its circumstances. He taught that pleasure was the chief end of life, but that the only pleasure worth having was a life of tranquillity, free from pain, disturbing passions, and above all, superstitious fears. The last-named led to Epicurus' theology. He was not exactly an atheist, for he taught that celestial beings existed, living in eternal calm, and caring nothing for the lives of men. Man, he taught, had no after-life for which to fear or hope. Let man, therefore, limit wants, desires, and aspirations to this life only, be satisfied with simple pleasures, and insulate himself from all the disturbances of public life, and private passion or ambition. The system of atomic physics, which Epicurus drew from Democritus, was incidental to this end, and an aid in his endeavour to eliminate divine agency in creation. In itself, as its great Latin exponent, Lucretius, shows, Epicureanism was not an ignoble cult. It was, nevertheless, a ready philosophic refuge for the hedonist and the sensualist who sought specious cover and excuse for self-indulgence.[1]

The *Stoics* (18) were philosophers who regarded Zeno, who taught in Athens around 300 BC, as their founder. The school

[1] See Cicero, *In Pisonem*.

had links with Tarsus, for a second Zeno, one of the early exponents of the system, came from there. The school, like that of Epicurus, was the fruit of the spirit's quest for a refuge and an escape from the impact of troublous times. Man should live, the Stoics taught, 'conformably to nature'. The highest expression of 'nature', in the sense in which the Stoics used it, was reason. To be virtuous, that is, to live in harmony with reason, was the only good; not to be virtuous was the only evil. All other things, life, death, pleasure, pain, were 'indifferent'. The Stoic, therefore, should be absolutely brave, knowing that pain and death are not evils; absolutely continent, knowing that pleasure is not a good; absolutely just, for he should be uninfluenced by prejudice or favour. The Stoics, in consequence, laid emphasis on the supremacy of the rational over the emotional in man, on individual self-sufficiency, which included the right to suicide, and on stern, unbending endurance. Stoicism had great attractions for the Roman mind, and produced the noble meditations on life and ethics of Seneca, Epictetus, and Marcus Aurelius. Its pantheistic view of God as a 'world-soul' also had its appeal for minds which rejected a cruder paganism, but found no rest in the doctrines of Epicurus. Its faults were a certain coldness, and a spiritual pride quite alien to the spirit of Christianity.

The occasion of Paul's address to the philosophers' distinguished company was not a trial in the judicial sense of the word. On the other hand, the Areopagus had certain rights in connection with public speaking, and it would have been unwise to treat lightly the invitation to speak. Verse 22 should be translated: 'Paul stood in the midst of the assembly' (cf. iv. 7). There was probably also a considerable listening audience of the type which has left a mark upon the oratory of more than one public speaker whose work has survived.

c. The sermon (xvii. 22–31)

This famous address is Paul's first major exposition of the gospel to an audience without a background of Old Testament theology or Jewish thought. Luke's report is, of course, a brief report of an address which must have been very much longer.[1]

i. The homiletics. Paul begins with an arresting statement: 'Athenians, I observe that in all respects you are an uncommonly religious people' (22). The av rendering *too superstitious* is a mistranslation. The phrase was not disrespectful but did contain a touch of irony which the audience would find challenging. Above the scene, and around, and comprehended in that sweep of the hand which was characteristic of Paul's oratory, were the famous shrines and gleaming statues of the Hellenic gods.

Like Christ Himself, Paul next attached his theme to a detail familiar to the experience of his hearers: 'For as I was passing through your city and noting the monuments of your devotion, I found also an altar dedicated to an "unknown god".' (The Greek text has no article; 'an' or 'the' could both be legitimately supplied.) There is plenty of evidence for such altars. Pausanias noticed altars 'to gods who are called unknown' on his way from Phalerum to Athens. Philostratus mentions altars at Athens 'to the unknown deities'. An altar has been found at Pergamum inscribed 'to the unknown deities'. Such altars had no special deity in view. The dedication was designed to ensure that no god was overlooked to the possible harm of the city.

In bold denial of the validity of the famous temples clustered round him, Paul then proceeded to state a fundamental doctrine (24–28), and to reinforce his point by a verse from the Stoic poet Aratus of Soli in Cilicia, Paul's native country. After the quotation he drives home his point again (29). Note now something subtle and in tune with the method of Paul on another famous occasion. In xxiii. 6, before the Sanhedrin, Paul divided his audience by appealing to one part. Here before him were Epicureans and Stoics. He rightly divined that the Stoic element was more open to his appeal. The determined materialism of the Epicurean listeners made

[1] J. B. Phillips has an interesting expanded version in an appendix to his translation of Acts. *The Young Church in Action*, pp. 100–103.

sympathetic contact difficult. It is notable that verses 24 and 28 are couched in Stoic language, and quote two Stoic poets, Aratus and Cleanthes, who both used the words. (Whether he was also quoting Epimenides, as Rendel Harris maintained,[1] cannot, in view of the paucity of the fragments, be determined.) In verse 29 the language is notably Stoic. To win a basis of agreement Paul lays no emphasis on the personality of God. 'We ought not to think', he says, 'that the divine nature (or "deity" in the abstract) is like gold, or silver, or stone. . . .' Stoicism was pantheistic; the listening crowd was polytheistic. Paul begins with the simplest platform common to both: there is something divine, which the religious strive to please, and some philosophers seek to comprehend.

It is the common fault of those who seek to commend the gospel to an alien or hostile audience by an adaptation of approach or a recasting of language, to lose the point of their appeal, and leave their hearers with no vital challenge. Paul avoided this error. In verse 30 he reaches his main point. The last words were a frontal attack.

ii. The doctrine. Note first the lofty view of God. God the Creator stands first, and is Jewish in conception (24; cf. Gn. i. 1; Ex. xx. 11; Is. xlv. 7; Ne. ix. 6). God is self-sufficient, and is the God who provides all good things (25; cf. Gn. ii. 7; Rom. viii. 32). *Life and breath* imply existence and its continuance. The equality of all men before Him follows (26). Paul had clashed with the Jews on this subject, and must have been aware that his words were challenging Gentile prejudices as strong. It was the boast of the Athenians that they had 'sprung from the soil'. The truth Paul put into these words cut at the root of all national pride, engendered by polytheism on the one hand and philosophic pride on the other. The Stoic, especially Seneca and Epictetus, had glimpsed the truth of the unity of mankind under God, but such philosophy lacked 'a lifting power'. '. . . It was not given to the Greek or to the Roman, but to the Jew, separated though he was from every

[1] See Ramsay, *The Teaching of Paul in Terms of the Present Day*, pp. 278, 279.

other nation, to safeguard the truth of the unity of mankind, and to proclaim the realization of the truth through the blood of a Crucified Jew.'[1]

Paul's view of sin, righteousness, and judgment is more bluntly expressed in the first three chapters of Romans. He is writing there to a body of believers. In the chapter before us he is speaking tactfully, but still uncompromisingly, to a thoughtful pagan audience. It is implied in Acts xvii that the pagan world had made little progress in searching for its Creator. In Romans it is more vigorously stated that, for all God's visible presence in His creation, the world at large had failed to find Him.

The call to repentance (30) would be equally unwelcome to Stoic and Epicurean; to the latter, because it would conflict not only with his denial of immortality but with his whole notion of the gods; to the former, because he regarded 'the wise man' as self-sufficient, who stood in no need of atonement, and need fear no judgment to come.

The resurrection is set forth as the final authentication of the message. Proof is not detailed, either because Luke abbreviated the end of the address, or because Paul was interrupted at this point.

d. The sequel (xvii. 32–34)

Did Paul regard his sermon as a success or a failure? Note that there was general rejection (32). The Epicureans were fanatical opponents of a doctrine of resurrection. The idea of immortality, which the Epicureans also rejected, would be generally held by the rest of the court and listening audience; but the notion of the body rising again, glorified in newness of life, was alien to them. So the Epicureans rudely *mocked*. More politely, the Stoics said, *We will hear thee again of this matter*. No church appears to have been founded in Athens, but there were converts (34), one of them a member of the court.

Ramsay[2] sums up: 'It would appear that Paul was dis-

---

[1] R. J. Knowling quoting Alford, *op. cit.*, II, 374.
[2] *St. Paul the Traveller and Roman Citizen*, p. 252.

appointed and perhaps disillusioned by his experience in Athens. He felt that he had gone at least as far as was right in the way of presenting his doctrine in a form suited to the current philosophy; and the result had been little more than naught. When he went on from Athens to Corinth he no longer spoke in the philosophic style. . . . Apparently the greater concentration of purpose and simplicity of method in his preaching at Corinth is referred to by Luke, when he says (Acts xviii. 5) that, when Silas and Timothy joined him, they found him wholly possessed by, and engrossed in the Word. This strong expression, so unlike anything else in Acts, must, on our hypothesis, be taken to indicate some specially marked character in the Corinthian preaching.' See especially, in support of this view, the first four chapters of 1 Corinthians. Note the categorical statement in ii. 1, 2, the touch of disillusionment in i. 18–25, and the tone of irony against philosophy which infuses all four chapters. Writing some eighteen years later (1913) Ramsay[1] considerably modifies this verdict. 'I went too far . . .' he says. 'I did not allow for adaptation to different classes of hearers, in one case the tradesmen and middle classes of Corinth, in the other the more strictly university and philosophic class in Athens.'

The result of the Athenian mission was to send Paul to Corinth for his major assault on the Greek world. The cosmopolitan port, set astride a major highway of trade, was, in fact, more promising as a sphere of evangelism than the intellectually proud and supercilious university town. Conybeare and Howson,[2] however, point to one result of Paul's visit to Athens which must not be overlooked. The speech itself, to borrow a phrase written by a great Athenian historian five centuries earlier, is 'no mere effort of the moment, but a possession for ever'.[3] It so happened that a profusion of great literature reveals to us the life of Athens, the power of her thought, the deep insights of her great minds, the vitality of her art and the

---

[1] *The Teaching of Paul in Terms of the Present Day*, pp. 110, 111.
[2] *The Life and Epistles of Saint Paul*, p. 296.
[3] Thucydides, i. 22.

nobility of her highest ideals. In this conspicuous passage of Scripture we hear the Jew of Tarsus, whom Glover called 'the greatest of the Greeks', address the Athenians with due respect for their achievements of thought, but calling them in polite speech ignorant idolaters, summoning them to repentance, and warning of judgment to come.

Additional Notes

xvii. 16. Paul's spirit *was stirred in him*. The word used is related to the noun discussed at xv. 39 and contains the notion of sharp emotional disturbance. It is *paroxuneto*, and a verb so vehement is a strong reminder of what idolatry, even in its most artistic form, meant to a Christian. Those who seek a Baedeker description of the multitude of idols in Athens will find a detailed catalogue in Pausanias' *Attica*. His account of the older glories of Athens is dated about a century later than Paul's visit, but little change could have taken place in the scene which provoked Paul's spirit.

xvii. 18. *This babbler*. The word applied (*spermologos*) refers both in Aristophanes and Aristotle to small active, granivorous birds. It formed a vivid metaphor in Demosthenes and Theophrastus, and, as this verse shows, in Athenian slang, for the philosophical Autolycus, the 'picker-up of trifles', alert, inquisitive, and ready both to snap up odd ideas and to retail them.

xvii. 22. Paul's use of the word translated *too superstitious* reveals his strong command of Attic Greek. It is *deisidaimonesteros*, and extant literature shows both a good and a bad sense. Aristotle used the word for genuine piety, the 'fear of the Lord' which is wisdom's first element. Theophrastus used it for superstition and this is the sense chosen by the AV. The better significance fits Paul's theme and apparent attitude, though, no doubt, a touch of irony left a point on the utterance.

xvii. 27. The word translated *feel after* would likewise raise echoes in the mind of the listeners, who would all be well acquainted with both Homer and Plato. Homer uses the word of Paul's metaphor (*Od.* ix. 416) for the groping of the blinded Cyclops seeking the entrance to his cave. Plato, like Paul, uses it figuratively in his noblest dialogue (*Phaedo*, 99B) for man's guesses at truth.

xvii. 28. The fragment of Cleanthes quoted runs:

'Thou, Zeus, art praised above all gods; many are thy names and thine is the power eternally. The origin of the world was from thee: and by law thou rulest over all things. Unto thee may all flesh speak, *for we are thy offspring*. Therefore will I raise a hymn unto thee: and will ever sing of thy might. The whole order of the heavens obeys thy word, as it moves round the earth, small and great luminaries commingled. How great thou art. King above all eternally. Nor is anything done on earth, apart from thee, nor in the firmament, nor in the seas save that which the wicked do by their own folly. But thine is the skill to set even the crooked straight; what is without shape is shaped and the alien is akin before thee. Thou hast fitted together all things in one, the good and evil together, that thy word should be one in all things abiding eternally. Let folly be dispersed from our souls, that we may repay the honour we have received of thee. Singing praise of thy works for ever as becometh the sons of men.'

Cleanthes, son of Phanius of Assos, was head of the Stoic School from 263 to 232 BC. Aratus of Soli in Cilicia (315–240 BC) likewise used the words in the fifth line of his *Phaenomena*, a poem on astronomy. It is impossible to say who used them first. The opening lines of the *Phaenomena* run: 'From Zeus let us begin; him do we mortals never leave unnamed; full of Zeus are all the streets and all the market-places of men; full is the sea and the havens thereof; always we all have need of Zeus. *For we are also his offspring*; and he in his kindness unto men giveth favourable signs and wakeneth the people to work, reminding them of livelihood. He tells what time the soil is best for the labour of the ox and for the mattock, and what time the seasons are favourable both for the planting of trees and for casting all manner of seeds. For himself it was who set the signs in heaven, and marked out the constellations, and for the year devised what stars chiefly should give to men right signs of the seasons, to the end that all things might grow unfailingly. Wherefore him do men ever worship first and last. Hail, O Father, mighty marvel, mighty blessing unto men.'

The evidence for a remoter quoting of Epimenides, the half-legendary Cretan bard and prophet of 500 BC, rests on the Syriac commentary of Isho'dad of Merv, in which these words are found: 'As certain of your own sages have said—Paul takes both of these from certain heathen poets. Now about this, "*In him we live*", etc.; because the Cretans said as truth about Zeus, that he was a lord, he was lacerated by a wild boar and buried; and behold, his grave is among us; so therefore Minos, son of Zeus, made a laudatory speech on behalf of his father; and he said in it, The Cretans carve a tomb for thee, O high and holy one! *Liars, evil beasts and slow bellies!* For thou art not dead for ever; thou art alive and risen; *for in thee we live and are moved and have our being*, so therefore the blessed Paul took this sentence from Minos; for he took again, "*We are the offspring of God*" from Aratus, the poet. . . .'

It will be noted that the passage includes a phrase which is used by Paul at Tit. i. 12, and Clement of Alexandria says that the words were from Epimenides the Cretan, who may, in consequence, have been the author of the whole poem quoted.

The fact that Luke's brief abstract of the speech contains so many echoes of classical authors, and Greek philosophy, is eloquent testimony to Paul's Greek education.

xvii. 30. Even in Elizabethan English *winked at* was an unfortunate translation, for even then it contained the notion of connivance. Toleration is all that can be postulated. The Greek quite literally says 'overlooked'.

XI. CORINTH (xviii. 1-28)

Corinth, the capital of Roman Greece, was a city old in story. Destroyed after a Roman siege in 146 BC, and refounded more conveniently to the sea by Julius Caesar, Corinth lay on a highway of trade. It was traversed by the travelling legions, and crowded by the agents of trade and commerce. It possessed, in consequence, all those vices which have ever haunted cosmopolitan ports. Superbly placed on her narrow isthmus, the city was inevitably rich. Her presiding deity, from the pagan pantheon, was Poseidon, god of the seas, under whose protection, in the days when Greek fought Greek before the Romans came, Corinth's fleets had sailed against the ships of Athens, and Corinth's merchantmen had sallied forth to compete with the Phoenicians for the trade of the inland seas. The great Isthmian games were held in Poseidon's honour, and have left a mark of metaphor on the ninth chapter of Paul's first letter to the Corinthian church. Above the ruins of the older city towered the 2,000-foot bulk of the Acrocorinthus, and here Aphrodite had her shrine, served by a host of priestess courtesans, who helped to give Corinth her rank flavour of immorality.

So notorious was the city for its debauchery that the phrase 'to play the Corinthian' found its place in Greek to express the lowest of loose living, and even in modern English 'a Corinthian' once meant a polished rake. Here, says G. G. Findlay,[1] Paul 'confronted the world's glory, and infamy with the sight of "Jesus Christ and Him crucified", confident that in the word of the Cross lay a spell to subdue the pride and cleanse the foulness of Corinthian life, a force which would prove to Gentile society in this place of its utter corruption the wisdom and power of God unto salvation. In "the Church of God in Corinth", with all its defects and follies, this redeeming power was lodged.'

a. The church founded (xviii. 1–11)

The founding of a Christian church at Corinth was one of the great achievements of Paul's life. At Athens, where the apostle first met the Greeks on their historic soil, the gospel had not met with wide success. Somewhat heavy in spirit, and the

[1] *Expositor's Greek Testament*, II, p. 734.

victim perhaps of one of his periodic illnesses (1 Cor. ii. 3; 1 Thes. iii. 7), Paul was in no condition to face the task presented by the great seaport town. If Ramsay is correct in diagnosing the 'thorn in the flesh' as a form of Asiatic malaria, it is possible to guess the nature of the 'weakness and fear and trembling' with which Paul faced his task. His appearance at the time, due no doubt to the ravages of illness, may not have been prepossessing, and some have read into such statements as 1 Cor. iv. 10 and 2 Cor. x. 1, 10, xii. 15 a suggestion that prejudice was thus excited among the aesthetically-minded Greeks.

Sustained, however, by a firm new friendship (xviii. 2, 3; Rom. xvi. 3) and heartened by the good news Silas and Timothy brought from Macedonia, Paul triumphed over his weakness, turned from the dissident synagogue, and under the shadow of Roman authority established the church in the wickedest of the Hellenic towns. It was a church, it appears, conspicuous for variety and activity (1 Cor. i. 4–8), consisting mainly of Gentiles, but containing converted Jews (1 Cor. i. 12, vii. 18, xii. 13). 'Not many wise, not many mighty, not many high-born' appear to have joined the fellowship, but there were some who fell under these heads, and the statement itself must be read in the context of subtle irony which colours the first four chapters of the first letter.[1] The impression is gained of an assembly marked by considerable contrasts of position and wealth. It contained certainly some of the sorrier dregs of the city.

A few of the converts, some indeed 'wise men after the flesh' and 'noble' (1 Cor. i. 26), are known to us by name—Crispus, the ruler of the synagogue, Erastus, the city treasurer (Rom. xvi. 23; and perhaps Acts xix. 22 and 2 Tim. iv. 20), Stephanas and Gaius, who seem to have been in a position to exercise generous hospitality, and the lady Chloe, who had a large household. Also mentioned are Fortunatus, Achaicus, Quartus, and Tertius who acted as amanuensis for the Epistle to the Romans. A strong Latin element appears likely.

[1] Ramsay, *The Teaching of Paul in Terms of the Present Day*, pp. 414–423.

It was a difficult congregation, as time was to show. In his study of the seven churches of Revelation, Ramsay has shown how a Christian community tends to reflect the defects and qualities of the society in which it is located. This is evidently true of Corinth. The turbulence and spirit of faction, the fundamental scepticism, the deplorable relapses, the undue tolerance towards sins of impurity, the intellectual arrogance and philosophical posing, and the very abuse of the gifts of the Spirit for self-display, which seem to have marred the Christian community, were reflections of the life of the restless Greek city itself. And yet, formed and moulded with care, this material, intractable though it was, proved of uncommon richness. The two long letters of Paul reflect this care on his part.

Verse 2 is confirmed by Suetonius,[1] who remarks that Claudius expelled the Jews from Rome because of rioting in the ghetto 'at the instigation of one Chrestos'. The reference is obviously to Christ, and as A. Momigliano[2] insists, those who deny that Suetonius made the simple mistake of confusing the two Greek words 'christos' and 'chrestos', a mistake aided by both semantics and phonetics, must undertake the difficult task of proving their contention. The Nazareth Decree, the significance of which has been vigorously debated by classical scholars, but curiously overlooked by Christian historians,[3] further confirms that Claudius was faced with problems arising from the first impact of the preaching of Christianity on the Jews of Rome. Claudius was an odd person, a sort of Roman James the First, who would have been much happier with his books than on the seat of imperial authority. Ancient historians persist in calling him mad, but the more Claudius' actual achievements are studied, the clearer becomes the impression that he was a man of learning, and of no mean ability. It is a fair guess that he was a spastic, whose faulty co-ordinations conveyed an impression of subnormality to the unsympathetic

[1] *Claudius*, xxv. 4.
[2] *The Emperor Claudius and His Achievement*, pp. 36, 37 and associated notes.
[3] For a brief account see E. M. Blaiklock, *Out of the Earth*, chapter III.

age in which he lived, and resulted, in his early years, in a ridicule and misunderstanding which damaged his personality.

If it is true that the seating in the synagogue was arranged according to trades and callings, Paul may have found his friends Aquila and Priscilla (2) because he had been trained in a craft indigenous to Cilicia, the manufacture of goat-hair cloth and tents.[1] The nature of such self-supporting evangelism is worth studying. Arriving at Corinth, Paul seems to have sought first for secular employment, and to have found in the trade and calling in which he, like all Jews, had been trained, a means of daily sustenance. From this point his common method was followed. He appealed first to the Jews (4). Few in the synagogues were like those he had recently met in Berea. A minority, frequently despised, often persecuted, fiercely proud and conscious of race, bitterly contemptuous of Gentile breeds without the Law, the Jews as a people, in Corinth as in Palestine, found it impossible to adapt their outlook to the thought that the faith which was emerging from Judaism was for the stranger equally with the Jew. Hence the familiar process of challenge, rejection, hatred, and violence (6).

b. The proconsul (xviii. 12–17)

On this occasion the persecutors struck an unusual magistrate, whose character Luke sketches in firm lines. He correctly describes Gallio (12) as a *deputy* or 'proconsul', and the vivid little story of the Roman is consistent with what is known from a few other sources[2] of his character and official attitude. Gallio was brother to Seneca and this brief encounter may have given rise to the legendary association of Seneca and Paul.

c. Paul's vow (xviii. 18–23)

Verses 18 to 23 form a strangely compact narrative. Luke appears anxious to hurry on to the next great scene of urban evangelism. We would gladly hear what happened at Cen-

---

[1] The Latin for hair-cloth is 'cilicium'.
[2] Collected by R. J. Knowling, *op. cit.*, II, pp. 389, 390.

chrea, and how Phoebe, deaconess of the Cenchrean church, won the praise Paul bestows upon her (Rom. xvi. 1, 2), but Luke for some reason chooses to omit all detail. Perhaps he finds a measure of embarrassment in what, after all, forms the puzzle of this portion of his story, to wit Paul's taking of a Nazarite vow after his rejection of Judaism. Whether such conformity involved the full ritual of Numbers vi is not clearly stated, but it is significant that Paul's vow is connected with a forthcoming visit to Jerusalem. In spite of his clear and uncompromising stand for an unfettered Christianity, Paul was always visibly anxious to conciliate the wary and sensitive Pharisaic wing of the Church, which was dominant at Jerusalem. Acts xxi shows how far he was prepared to go in the demonstration of his loyalty to tradition, and the vow, and doubtless the dedication of hair in the temple, may have been a similar and earlier act of goodwill. If so, it seems to have failed in its object. The name of Jerusalem is not mentioned, and the narrative, derived, no doubt, from Paul's own report, hurries on to the beginning of the third journey as though the Jerusalem interlude was an unpleasant memory. There was evidently no warm welcome there, and the ex-Pharisee's conformity did nothing to allay suspicion.

d. Apollos (xviii. 24-28)

It is clear that, anxious to carry on the religious policy of Augustus whom he profoundly admired, Claudius was deeply informed about, and genuinely interested in the religious situation in the Mediterranean world. Such interest, in fact, may not be without reference to this story of Apollos. A long letter of the emperor's has survived in which he seeks to regulate the serious Jewish problems of Alexandria. This document, discovered among the papyri in 1920, appears to contain the first secular reference to Christian missionaries.[1] It was written in AD 41, and expressly forbids the Alexandrian Jews 'to bring or invite other Jews to come by sea from Syria. If they do not abstain from this conduct', Claudius threatens, 'I shall proceed

[1] For other references in Acts to nameless missionaries see xi. 19, xxviii. 15.

against them for fomenting a malady common to the world.'

Apollos, therefore, may have had much in common with Aquila and Priscilla, his host and hostess at Ephesus. All three had, it appears, come under the unfavourable notice of the authorities because of their Christian testimony. Such decrees of banishment as that recorded in verse 2 were seldom completely or consistently enforced. Aquila and Priscilla had decided to take the Emperor seriously, and seeking an environment for their trade similar to that which they had found in Rome, had emigrated first to Corinth, where Christianity enjoyed comparative liberty and toleration (12-17) and then moved on with Paul to Ephesus (19). Apollos, perhaps because authority in Alexandria interpreted the Claudian rescript of 41 in the spirit of the metropolitan decision of 49, found himself under similar constraint to emigrate. These verses give, perhaps, the key to 1 Cor. iii. 4. Apollos probably lacked that emphasis on the atoning death which marked Paul's gospel. Aquila and Priscilla more accurately instructed him, but his less mature viewpoint may have persisted in some of the members of the Christian community, as 'John's baptism' was found to be persisting across the Aegean.

Additional Notes

xviii. 4 and 8. Imperfect tenses in these verses point to the consistent and industrious evangelism of Paul. 'He used to debate in the synagogue every sabbath, and press his message on the Jews and Greeks . . . and many of the Corinthians who heard him would believe and be baptized.'

xviii. 5. Readings vary between 'he was constrained in spirit', and 'he was constrained by the Word'. In sum, the meaning is the same. Paul felt the urgency of the gospel on his heart. The brevity of time, the magnitude of the task, a sense of weakness, and withal of responsibility, all these, together with a consciousness of God's indwelling power, led to a change of method. Instead of *reasoning* (4) Paul now *testified*. Exactly what this means is difficult to say. Personal experience is certainly the keynote of the later speeches in the book. Perhaps 1 Cor. ii. 1–4 refers to this simplification of his message.

xviii. 6. The symbolism of 'shaking out one's raiment' is seen in Ne. v. 13, where the same phrase occurs. It is figurative of renunciation and the casting off of all contact. Compare the story in Polybius (iii. 33).

xviii. 18. It is fair to note that grammatically the sentence could be construed to mean that *Aquila* had 'shaved his head'. All authorities, however, appear to agree that the best interpretation is that Paul, and not his companion, had taken the vow. This is in tune with the preoccupation of verse 21.

XII. EPHESUS (xix. 1–41)

Ephesus was an old Ionian foundation at the mouth of the Cayster river-valley. The cities which sprang from the colonies of the Greeks dot the coastline of the Mediterranean and the Black Sea, and were fundamentally trading-posts. Generally a migrant community of Greeks did not seek to dominate the hinterland, but to secure an easily defended harbour and adjacent coastline as a bridge-head of trade. A colony was, in fact, called an 'emporion' or 'way in'. Great cities grew from such foundations, Marseilles, for example, and Ephesus herself. Under the compulsions of history some of the colonial cities became the capitals of kingdoms, Syracuse, for example, and Alexandria. And in all cases colonies became the centre of urban cultures, distinctive, dynamic, and civilizing.

Ephesus had been founded to command one of the highways of Asia Minor. The great blunt peninsula, which thrusts westward towards Europe, was once, before the ancient folly of deforestation stripped its hillsides, choked its harbours, and changed its climate, a teeming and a fertile land. Snow-capped ranges looked over green valleys, down which the great trade routes from Asia ran to the Inland Sea. Land-locked harbours indented the rugged coastline, and busy trade thronged the cities which clustered on road and seaway. Two hundred and thirty separate communities in Asia Minor of Roman times, each proud of its individuality and wealth, issued their own coinage and managed their own affairs.

Queen among these communities was Ephesus. Built near the site of the shrine of an old Anatolian fertility goddess, the Ionian city had become the seat of an Oriental cult. The Anatolian deity had been taken over by the Greeks under the name of Artemis, or Diana as the Romans called her. Grotesquely represented with turreted head and many breasts the goddess and her cult found expression in a vast and famous temple, served, like that of Aphrodite at Corinth, by a host of priestess courtesans.

Round the cult clustered much trade. Ephesus became the place of pilgrimage for tourist-worshippers, all eager to carry away talisman and souvenir. Hence the prosperous guild of the silversmiths, whose livelihood consisted in the making of the silver shrines or models of the temple which visitors bought to carry home. Ephesus, in fact, leaned more and more on the trade which came with religion and superstition. There is evidence that even in Paul's day the harbour, now separated from the sea by twenty miles of reedy marshland, was silting up. Paul's ship in AD 57 made no call there. Ephesus boasts on a special coin that she was the landing-place for the galleys which bore Roman officials to Asia; but that is not to say that the heavier type of galley which carried the merchandise of trade was not already finding the splendid harbour of Smyrna a more convenient and commodious haven. An attempt to improve the channel was made, Tacitus[1] tells us, in 65 BC, but local determination slackened as the task proved too daunting, and matters were left once more to take their course. In Paul's day, the once famous harbour was on its way to becoming the reedy swamp whose rustling under the evening wind seemed so uncanny to Sir William Ramsay.[2] Ephesus ceased to be a port, its trade declined, and life went out of the city.

Ephesus, for all her past splendour, was a dying city, pre-occupied with parasite pursuits, living, like Athens, on a

---

[1] *Ann.* xvi. 23. [2] *The Seven Churches*, p. 214.

reputation, and a curious meeting-place of old and new religions, of superstition and philosophy, of East and West. Her 'lampstand' is gone from its place, for Ephesus' disease was mortal, and it is possible to detect in the letter to Ephesus in the Apocalypse a touch of that lassitude which was abroad in the town, and which infected the church.

a. The Ephesian church (xix. 1–20)

i. The twelve disciples (xix. 1–7). This curious incident forms a preface to the story of the founding of the Ephesian church. Luke's reasons for recording it may be as follows. First, it seems clear that the little group at Ephesus (Luke emphasizes the fact, in verse 7, that they were no more than twelve in number) were a relic of Apollos' immature ministry in the city (xviii. 24, 25). Even after his salutary meeting with Aquila and Priscilla, and his frank acceptance of the Pauline gospel, Apollos' message and personality had a distinctiveness which tended to collect a personal following (1 Cor. iii. 4). Paul deplored such sectarianism, and it may have been important to set on record the inadequacy of the pre-Pauline theology at Ephesus. Secondly, Paul's global ministry is now Luke's whole theme. Nothing is known of the streams of Christian witness which flowed parallel and apart from his, but those streams were undoubtedly numerous, sometimes apostolic, and quite certainly effective. It is further clear that it was Paul's liberal view of the gospel, and not the Judaistic version, which prevailed in all Gentile churches, not only in those founded directly or indirectly by Paul himself and his immediate associates. Luke may therefore have felt constrained to tell the story of one group of disciples who gladly abandoned an intermediate position when presented with a fuller gospel.

The point at issue need not have been spiritual gifts, of the sort whose value and significance Paul is obviously anxious not to over-emphasize in his first letter to the Corinthian Christians. Something about the small group which welcomed him at Ephesus aroused his curiosity. Perhaps they were marked by an asceticism inherited from the Baptist. Perhaps they held a doctrine of sin and a repentance which lacked assurance, and that sense of emancipation which Christ, rather than John, bestowed. As disciples of John the Baptist they could hardly have lacked knowledge of the Holy Spirit (see, for example, Jn. i. 33). What they did lack was that glad consciousness of the Comforter's active presence. The RV translation '. . . whether the Holy Ghost was given' should be preferred. They did not doubt the existence of the Third Person of the Trinity, but were without knowledge whether the promised baptism had taken place. Finally, says Luke, note the number of those who were involved. It is impossible to imagine that the Ephesian church had considerable roots apart from those sent down in the firm earth of Paul's two years of ministry.

ii. Signs and wonders (xix. 8–20). The old sequence of events unfolded, monotonously true to form. It was not lack of sad experience which led Paul in chapters ix–xi of the Epistle to the Romans to speak of the national rejection of Christ by the people privileged first to hear of Him. It was an essential part of Luke's theme to underline that fact. Hence the careful record of Paul's method, his scrupulous regard for the synagogue, his programme of patient teaching and persuasion, the crystallizing of opposition, and the altogether justifiable 'turning to the Gentiles'.

It seems that, when the gospel moved abroad in Gentile Ephesus, there was a reception quite in accord with the spirit of the city. The place was a hot-bed of Oriental magic and superstition, and it is quite inevitable that, for both good and ill, such preoccupations should find a Christian interpretation, especially in the early days of the witness and experience of the Church. It is notable that there is no word of commendation from the lips of Paul or the pen of Luke for the practices recorded in verse 12.

The story of the sons of Sceva further illustrates the situation in the superstition-ridden town. The criminal fringe of Jewry has already twice found a place in the story in the person of such charlatans as Simon and Elymas, who used the prestige of Judaism to impose upon the credulous, and share the profits of the 'Chaldaeans and magicians', who were so often expelled from Rome.[1] Christianity itself has not been without experience of such camp-followers. The incident here described is beyond ready explanation in natural or psychological terms. The Jewish magic-mongers were tampering with forces beyond their knowledge, and paid the penalty of such rashness. R. J. Knowling[2] remarks: '. . . . it is surely a mark of truthfulness that the narrative ends where it does; a forger, we may well believe, would have crowned the story by a picture of the man, after baffling the imposters, healed by the word or touch of Paul.'

b. The guilds (xix. 21–41)

This admirably written story is a study in mob psychology. The scene, says Ramsay,[3] 'is the most instructive picture of society in an Asian city which has come down to us'. We are 'taken direct into the artisan life of Ephesus, and all is so characteristic, so true to common life, and so unlike what would occur to anyone writing at a distance, that the conclusion is inevitable: we have here a picture drawn from nature. . . .' The howling crowd, so typical of crowds the world over (32); the chanted invocation; the cool official cleverly controlling a most difficult situation (35–41); all these details ring true, and point to the report of an eyewitness, vivid and ironical. Moreover, as Ramsay continues, in the guildmaster's subtle and malicious speech (25–27) 'are concentrated most of the feelings and motives which, from the beginning to the end, made the mob so hostile to the Christians in the great oriental cities.'

In fact, in this chapter, sometimes dismissed by critics[4] as

---

[1] Tacitus, *Hist.* i. 22, *sup. cit.*, p. 104.

[2] *Op. cit.*, II, pp. 407, 408.

[3] *St. Paul the Traveller and Roman Citizen*, pp. 277, 278. *The Church in the Roman Empire*, VII, 5.

[4] E.g. C. S. C. Williams, *The Acts of the Apostles* (Black's Commentaries), p. 219, quoting W. L. Knox.

'of poor quality', we have some of Luke's most vivid and characteristic writing, and the description to boot of a situation which throws much light on the manner and motives of persecution against the early Church. Circumstances tally remarkably with those described some seventy years later in two extant letters[1] by Pliny, then Roman Governor of Bithynia, who was constrained to consult Trajan on certain pressing problems in his province arising from the growing strength of the Christian Church. It seems clear that the Governor was under pressure from two groups, the temple priests who found their shrines deserted, and the guild of butchers whose 'sacrificial meat', that subject of social difficulty in the Corinth church, was losing customers. It was the same situation as that which Luke so vividly describes in the chapter under review. The story shows that the Christian was at odds with society before he clashed with the State, and that a strong element in the first persecution of the Church was the trade guild, which found in the awkward and unaccommodating minority a threat to profit and an occasion of economic disturbance.[2]

The guilds, and the problem they presented to the non-conforming Christian, haunt the background of the New Testament. They were societies not trade unions, primarily social, and multitudinous in ancient society. Records exist of guilds of bankers, doctors, architects, producers of woollen and linen goods, dyers, workers in metal, stone or clay, builders, carpenters, pastry cooks, barbers, embalmers and transport workers. 'No other age', writes S. Dill,[3] 'felt a deeper craving for some form of social life, greater than the family, but narrower than the state.' Formed under this gregarious urge, the trade guilds satisfied the need of the people at large for social intercourse and self-expression. On the other hand, the tumult at Ephesus shows that the social club, under adroit

---

[1] *Ep.* x. 96, 97.

[2] The whole question is briefly discussed in the Tyndale New Testament Lecture for 1951, *The Christian in Pagan Society*, by E. M. Blaiklock.

[3] *Roman Society from Nero to Marcus Aurelius*, pp. 267, 271.

leadership such as it found in Demetrius, could be used as a sharp political weapon. Hence the sensitiveness of the Roman administration on the whole subject, and the severe laws about illegal association. It will be observed that the guild of the silversmiths secured its prime object. Paul, if we read the story rightly, was on the eve of withdrawal, but the scene in the theatre made sure that he would go, and no doubt placed the Christian group which he left behind him in a very embarrassing situation indeed.

An ambition was, however, fulfilled, and a stage in Paul's strategy of imperial evangelism completed. Beginning with the great cities of Southern Galatia, Paul was at first eager to reach Ephesus. That intention may be fairly divined from the story. He was diverted from this goal for a time by God's clear guidance (xvi. 6-8), and led to pass over into Europe. Ephesus, none the less, was in Paul's mind a link between East and West, a gate between the continents, and Paul's purpose never wavered to establish a strong witness there. 'After he had planted his banner in Ephesus', writes Ramsay,[1] 'he had established his line of communication firmly along the great road which led to the capital of the Empire.' It was then that he announced: *I must also see Rome* (xix. 21). And a little later, thinking of the great province of the west, he told the Roman church (Rom. xv. 24, 28) 'I will come by you into Spain'. In the same chapter he speaks of labour in Illyricum, Macedonia, and Achaia. 'That is the language', Ramsay continues, 'not of a mere enthusiast, but of a general and a statesman who plans out the conquest of the Empire. He talks of provinces, and as he marches on his victorious course he plants his footsteps in their capitals.'

A little more is known of the progress of the Ephesian church from the record of the New Testament. No church was more closely associated with famous names. Timothy seems to have been commissioned by Paul towards the end of his career to do some special work in Ephesus (1 Tim. i. 3). From various statements about John Mark it may be inferred that he had

[1] *Pauline Studies*, p. 198.

something to do with the Asian group of churches, of which Ephesus was the chief (Col. iv. 10; 2 Tim. iv. 11; 1 Pet. v. 13). John was the church's guide and bishop in the years following the fall of Jerusalem. In Paul's Epistle to the Ephesians is seen the depth of spiritual understanding which Paul expected of those to whom he had ministered for over two years. In John's cryptic letter (Rev. ii. 1–7) is read the record of some weariness in witness but a soundness of doctrine which was proof against the subtle seductions of the party of pagan compromise (Rev. ii. 6).

Additional Notes

xix. 10. It has been alleged that the 'three years' of xx. 31 conflicts with this estimate. But the 'three months' of verse 8 must be taken into account. Paul ministered in Ephesus for two full years and part of a third, and in speaking of time it was common practice to reckon even small fractions as wholes. By *Asia* in this verse proconsular Asia is meant, the political, not the geographical division. The province occupied the western end of the peninsula.

xix. 12. The words for *handkerchiefs* and *aprons* are Latin words, and evidence of the strong Roman element in the Greek city.

xix. 14. The 'chief priests' here mentioned are probably the family heads of the 'courses' of the Levites. Sceva is a Latin name, but there is nothing to show whether the father was a renegade from his post of Levitical dignity, or whether his sons only had soiled the fair name.

xix. 19. It is idle to estimate the value of the bonfire in terms of modern money. Save for the famous edict of Diocletian, which does relate wages and prices, and a few scattered scraps of similar information, we have little clear evidence of the purchasing power of money in the ancient world. It is obviously in terms of purchasing power that an estimate of the value of *fifty thousand pieces of silver* would be illuminating, and it is quite impossible to fix such a comparative figure. The commentators who have sedulously endeavoured to do so have wasted their arithmetic.

xix. 24. 'Demetrios, son of Menophilos, son of Tryphon of the thousand Boreis', has emerged from an Ephesian inscription. Ramsay[1] discusses the fair case which can be made for identifying this person with the person of the text. The *silver shrines* were probably models of the temple, and used for souvenirs, talismans, burial offerings, and dedicatory gifts by pilgrims. The translation should follow RV, 'no little business', rather than *no small gain*, though the twain necessarily coincided.

xix. 31. The *chief of Asia*, or the Asiarchs, were considerable officials, and Ramsay discusses at some length, in the chapter noted above, the obscure subject of their favourable attitude towards Paul. No firm conclusion is possible, but the fact, mentioned thus, in a chapter so evidently based on first-hand information, stands beyond dispute.

xix. 35. The image was probably a piece of meteoric debris.

xix. 38. The phrase *there are deputies* is typical of the cool, deprecating manner of this thoroughly capable official. 'There is, after all,' he says, 'a proconsul.'

xix. 39. In chapter viii of his *Pauline Studies*, an essay on 'the lawful assembly', Ramsay shows that the AV rendering is to be preferred to the RV. The Secretary of State for Ephesus (Ramsay's rendering of the title) makes the point that the assembly (*ekklēsia*) is not legally constituted, and liable to be classed as riotous by a sensitive Roman Government. The official assumes there is cause for complaint, but if Demetrius and his associates sought, for example, some restriction on the activities of aliens, the business should be on the agenda of the duly-constituted assembly with the proconsul in the chair. Only this assembly had power to transact business. Trajan's reply to Pliny's question about establishing a fire-brigade in

---

[1] *The Church in the Roman Empire*, pp. 112–145.

Nicomedia is a fair comment on the official attitude which made the Ephesian official uneasy. 'It is to be remembered', wrote the emperor, 'that societies of this sort have greatly disturbed the peace of the province. . . . Whatever name we give them, and for whatever purpose they may have been founded, they will not fail to transform themselves into factious assemblies. . . .' (Ep. x. 33, 34).

XIII. THE ROAD TO JERUSALEM (xx. 1–xxi. 15)

a. Farewell to Greece (xx. 1–6)

After the tumult in Ephesus Paul left the city, probably in the congenial company of Aquila and Priscilla, who are found active in Rome some months later (Rom. xvi. 3–5). Paul there speaks warmly of dire risks the couple had run for him. The apostle himself made for Macedonia. The record of the next ten months of arduous work is strangely brief. Luke, of course, was not aware that he was writing a major document of Church history. He recounted to Theophilus what he thought important, but especially what he knew from personal participation. He may also have regarded the visit to Europe, in spite of its westward direction, the prelude and preliminary to the return journey to Jerusalem, which was to prove so momentous. If Paul's chief object was to organize the collection for Jerusalem, on which he pathetically pinned the most ardent hopes, the visit to Greece was, in fact, such a prelude. It is of the nature of Christian work that those tasks, which appear at the time to be secondary, prove, in the outcome, to be more directly and fruitfully the labours of the Lord.

Paul's movements over this ill-recorded period may be to some extent surmised from the highly autobiographical second letter to the Corinthian church, which was written at the time. From this document it becomes clear that Paul left Ephesus in great distress, and came to Troas (2 Cor. i. 8–ii. 12). The mention of an opportunity for witness (ii. 12) in this place, where he had earlier been prevented from preaching, suggests that the apostle, in spite of anxiety over the non-arrival of Titus, spent a period of time there in the work of evangelism. He was anxious to receive Titus' report from Corinth, for the reception by that difficult congregation of his last letter still concerned him. He moved on to Philippi (ii. 13), hearing, no doubt, that Titus proposed to meet him there. His anxiety proved groundless, for Titus came to Macedonia with comforting news (vii. 5–16), and it was in this mood of relief that Paul wrote the first seven chapters of his second letter. But Corinth had lagged in the matter which was close, at this time, to Paul's heart, and Paul adds two more chapters (viii and ix) in order to stir the laggards to life and interest. Titus was sent again with the second letter, and with him on the embassy 'the brother, whose praise is in the gospel throughout all the churches' (viii. 6, 16, 17, 18, 22). This may be Luke himself. A third brother, 'many times proved earnest in many things', also accompanied the party. The abrupt opening of chapter x with a theme pursued to the end of chapter xiii, suggests that news came from Corinth at this point of a personal attack on Paul. The Judaizing missionaries had arrived, perhaps fresh from their mischief in Galatia.

Such were some of the preoccupations of this summer and autumn. Simultaneously Paul was preaching and organizing. He went through *those parts* (2), visiting the old centres of evangelism, and perhaps including the journey into Illyricum of which he speaks in Rom. xv. 19. A major item of business must have been the collection, and the appointment of delegates to carry it. With the approach of winter Paul, with Timothy and others, went down to Corinth, as he had planned to do (1 Cor. xvi. 6). Here for three months (3) he lodged with Gaius (Rom. xvi. 23), and wrote the Epistle to the Romans. The ministry in Corinth is reflected in the teaching of this document, and from the comparative serenity of its tone it may be inferred that Paul was victorious over those who had sought to harm his reputation and impugn his gospel.

Paul was conscious of a certain completeness in this portion of his ministry, and determined to make his departure for

Jerusalem a farewell to Greece. But the Corinthian Jews, still smarting from their humiliation in Gallio's court, remained bitterly vindictive, and news was unearthed of a plot to kill the apostle on the pilgrim ship to Ephesus. It is not impossible that throughout the world at this time Jewish feeling was heating like some subterranean fire towards the flash-point of the volcanic explosion of AD 66. Paul, the Roman citizen who claimed his rights, the cosmopolitan and imperially-minded evangelist, may have been to them a symbol of the collaboration with Rome which nationalistic passion held in contempt. Paul himself was apprehensive. He had recently asked the Roman church for the aid of their prayers against this very menace (Rom. xv. 30, 31). The Gentile Christians saw the peril clearly, and did their utmost to dissuade the apostle from the journey. 'In every city' (xx. 23) they warned him. All Paul would consent to do was to change his route, cancel his project of going aboard the pilgrim ship, and make a detour through familiar Macedonia. It is impossible not to be impressed by his firm determination to present the gifts of the Gentile Christians personally at Jerusalem. It was his last and supreme attempt to bind together in the bonds of love the two parts of the Church. In such cement he most devoutly trusted. To this ministry he refers in xx. 24. Paul's was not the first heart Jerusalem had broken (Lk. xix. 41). A considerable party of delegates, including Luke himself (*us* in verse 5), was reunited at Troas. It had been ten to twelve months of tremendous labour, writing, preaching, travelling, organizing. We would gladly know more about it. From now on the story becomes detailed and intimate.

b. Troas again (xx. 7-12)

Much concerning the practice of the early Church has been surmised from verse 7. The *first day* seems to have been set apart for the business of God (1 Cor. xvi. 2). In Troas it was an evening service culminating in a common meal. The gathering was held in an *upper chamber* (8), rendered *coenaculum*, or 'dining-room', in the Latin versions. The use of a private house for Christian purposes is notable. The sermon was a major item in the programme. The lamps have no ritual significance. It is perfectly obvious why Luke mentions them. The burning oil was the main reason for the deterioration of the atmosphere, most apparent higher in the room, where the unfortunate Eutychus sat in the window-alcove.

It is surely the physician who picks from the first experiences of his renewed fellowship with Paul the case of the young man Eutychus. The story is told with that reserve which might mark a medical report of the restoration of a dying patient in a modern clinic. Luke appears to vouch for the death of the youth, and it is easy to envisage the situation. Paul was lost in his theme, and must have been overwhelmed with horror and pity when an earnest lad, worn out with the long day's toil, and half-suffocated in the oil-laden air, was unable to keep awake. In a surge of agonized love the apostle's faith rose to the challenge, and death was defeated. The meeting continued, sustained by the passionate interest of Christians who as yet had no New Testament.

c. On to Miletus (xx. 13-16)

In a few business-like words Luke takes his readers over some of the most storied coasts of ancient myth and history. Troas was hard by the mound of ruins which marked the windy plain of Homer's Troy. The record of the three thousand years of occupation of that strategic site was already locked away in the stratified debris awaiting Schliemann and the modern archaeologist. Mitylene and Miletus had played notable parts in Ionian and Athenian history. The reader is left puzzled why Paul *had appointed* (13) to go afoot across the headland by way of the Roman road to Assos in Mysia. The story of chapter xxvii does not suggest that Paul was a bad sailor and disliked the passage round Cape Lectum. It is more probable that he was heavy with thought and desired solitude. He had been warned solemnly against the course he was taking, and may have wished to be alone with his prayers. Indeed it may be possible to penetrate a little more deeply into the apostle's mind. Luke remembered the pattern of his 'former treatise', how the narrative had covered over thirty years, and then had paused and lingered over the events of one week and one momentous period of three days. His second book was not unlike in shape. The narrative was to linger over events in Jerusalem which were in substance a 'passion' of Paul. Those events were preceded by a 'steadfast going up' to Jerusalem. Perhaps Paul himself saw this analogy, and consciously treading in the path of his Master sought the solitude of a journey on foot before the last lap of his pilgrimage.

d. At Miletus (xx. 17-38)

This is the only speech in the book which it is certain that Luke actually heard spoken. It is interesting to note the marks of accurate reporting. Luke's common method is to give a speech in outline, and generally to employ for that purpose his own diction. The charge to the Ephesian elders is marked throughout by Pauline expressions which can be matched in the Epistles. There are, for example, the following echoes in the text: Rom. i. 1, Phil. i. 1, Tit. i. 1 (19); 2 Cor. ii. 4 (19); 1 Cor. x. 33 (20); 2 Tim. iv. 7, 1 Tim. i. 12 (24); 1 Cor. xi. 23 (24); 2 Cor. vii. 2 (26); Col. iv. 17, 1 Tim. iv. 16, Eph. i. 14 (28); 2 Tim. iv. 5, Col. i. 12, and 28 (32); Rom. xv. 1 (35). (R. B. Rackham[1] develops this theme.) The linguistic evidence works in both directions, authenticates the speech, and authenticates the Epistles. Apart from this, the speech is vividly personal in tone. Verse 19, for example, is Paul's picture of himself, and squares with the personality of the Epistles. 'The narrative in Acts', writes A. W. F. Blunt,[2] 'has told us nothing of "tears"; it pictures Paul as the man who is always equal to a public emergency; Paul himself knows more of the private depressions and discouragements which he had to live through.'

From the speech emerges a clear picture of the ministry in Ephesus. Note the following: First, Paul's urgent faithfulness.

[1] *Op. cit.*, pp. 384, 385, 389-396 *passim*.
[2] *Op. cit.*, p. 231.

He was no seeker after popularity or the public's approval. Set like Ezekiel to a watchman's task, he discharged his duty with honest zeal and character to back his speech. Second, his loving sympathy. He was not the man to take words of doom upon his lips without emotion. Third, his indefatigable evangelism. Publicly and from house to house, in the city and throughout the province, he had preached the gospel, founding probably the 'seven churches'. Fourth, his independence. He was determined that no-one should ever say that he lived by the preaching of truth. Fifth, his insight. With clear foreknowledge he saw the shape of trouble and apostasy to come. John's letters to the Asian circuit in Revelation ii and iii show how true was Paul's forecast of events. Sixth, his wisdom. He left the Church efficiently organized and, as far as human organization could guard against trouble, he left constituted leaders, duly warned and strengthened against subversion, to meet and solve problems yet to be.

e. Across to Palestine (xxi. 1–15)

By a series of straight runs the ship continued its course through parts rich in history, to Cos, Rhodes, and Patara. It was an old established route mentioned by both Livy[1] and Lucan.[2] Ramsay[3] points out that the 'legs' of the journey were at the dictation of a nexus of daytime winds. The ship lay up at night. Patara, on the coast of Lycia, was the regular departure-point for the straight run across to Palestine or Egypt. At this time there was probably something near to daily sailings on the route. The party transhipped at Patara[4] for the 400-mile voyage, which was probably accomplished in three or four days. The ship must have been a galley of considerable size to require seven days for its unloading (3, 4).

The ancient Phoenician port (2, 3) was an old scene of

---

[1] xxxvii. 16.
[2] viii. 109, 246–248.
[3] *St. Paul the Traveller and Roman Citizen*, p. 293.
[4] Freya Stark, in *Ionia* and *The Lycian Shore* (*passim*), gives an interesting account of the area in recent times.

Hellenistic evangelism, where Paul had once before found acceptance with his report of work among the Asian Gentiles (xv. 3). The series of warnings which Paul appears to have regarded as a temptation to swerve from his purpose was here continued (4). Leaving Tyre after a warm farewell, the party passed to Ptolemais, the modern Acre, and thence to Caesarea, where Philip had settled twenty years before. Philip had a family of grown-up daughters who occupied a position of importance in the spiritual ministry of the local church. For Luke the historian this contact with the famous preacher was of prime importance.

Hereupon Agabus, of previous mention (xi. 27, 28), appeared, and with a symbolism reminiscent of an Old Testament prophet (e.g. Jeremiah xiii) repeated the warning which Paul's party, by this time, were finding profoundly disturbing. The Caesarean congregation added their own entreaties (12) as did Luke himself ('we', in verse 14). Paul's face was set to go to Jerusalem, and it is one of the puzzles of this chapter whether he was right in persisting. He was moving forward under a deep inner compulsion, and it is not for anyone lightly to question the honest convictions of such a man. At the same time great men are not beyond the possibility of error, and Scripture is habitually frank in reporting faults and failings. The question therefore remains open. Certain it is that a ministry all too short, to speak in human terms, was tragically abbreviated by the events which took place in Jerusalem, and which silenced the great voice of the apostle for vital years.

At the time, as was remarked above, Paul was perhaps conscious of a spiritual parallel with the pilgrimage of his Master. Perhaps he regarded Caesarea as his temptation and Gethsemane. If so, the congregation, catching the thought, echoed the garden prayer of Christ: *The will of the Lord be done* (14). R. B. Rackham[1] points out that Christ three times spoke of His own coming passion—three times Paul was warned. Beyond this Rackham perhaps presses the parallel too far.

[1] *Op. cit.*, p. 401.

Additional Notes

xx. 2. *When he had gone over those parts*, says AV. The same verb is rendered 'go through' in xiii. 6. There are nine examples in Acts, the only other occurrence of the verb being at 1 Cor. xvi. 5. It means to make a missionary journey, over or through the area named. In this verse *Greece* is used for the geographically more exact 'Achaia' (cf. xviii. 12). Luke is using the popular term in general use.

xx. 9. The AV translation is a little clumsy. Luke notes the boy's struggle with drowsiness, and his final collapse. 'Sitting in a window was a boy named Eutychus who was being borne down by deep sleep as Paul went on and on talking. Finally overcome by slumber he fell down from the third story and was picked up dead.'

xx. 15. Nautical terms are used. 'Sailing thence on the morrow we reached a point on the mainland over against Chios. On the next day we struck across to Samos.'

xx. 19. The noun rendered *humility of mind* is a characteristically Pauline word. It occurs five times in the Epistles. In Classical Greek the word is coloured by connotations of contempt. Christ ennobled 'meekness' and the words which expressed the idea.

xx. 20, 27. A verb used in both these verses for 'keeping back' or 'shunning' contains the idea of reefing sail. Paul was just ashore, and below in the port the sails of ships flapped drying in the breeze. Fresh from the sailor's speech and conversations, Paul puts a touch of salty vividness into his claim to have told them the whole counsel of God. 'I have not trimmed my sails in preaching truth to you.'

xx. 28. The word translated *overseers* (*episkopoi*) is the term which gave ultimately the word 'bishop'. It occurs five times in the New Testament, and on four of these occasions (Phil. i. 1; 1 Tim. iii. 2; Tit. i. 7 and the present passage) it refers to officers of the Christian Church. Peter (1 Pet. ii. 25) applies it to Christ. In the Septuagint, and generally in Hellenistic

Greek, it means overseers and commissioners of all types (e.g. the minor officials of Ne. xi. 9, 14, and 2 Ki. xi. 18). It is not to be supposed that at this stage the word indicated a clearly defined class of leadership, distinct, for example, from the deacons. At the same time this passage does contain the notion of spiritual guidance and leadership later associated with the bishop's office.

xxi. 3. 'Showing up Cyprus', says Luke, remembering vividly the moment when the blue heights of the island rose suddenly from the sea.

xxi. 6. *They returned home*. Literally the phrase runs 'returned to their own things'. This is the only rendering Greek has for the peculiarly English expression 'home'. It is curious that the AV was not bold enough to translate similarly another context where the same phrase occurs. Jn. i. 11 reads literally thus: 'He came to His own things and His own people did not receive Him'; i.e. 'He came home and His own folk turned Him from the door'.

xxi. 9. Jeremy Taylor's work on the 'Liberty of Prophesying' was written, not to uphold the liberty of prediction, but of preaching. This was the Elizabethan use.

XIV. AT JERUSALEM (xxi. 16–xxiii. 35)

a. Paul's compromise (xxi. 16–26)

The brethren, writes Luke, *received us gladly* (17). James was in undisputed control of the powerful Jerusalem church, and officially received the considerable contributions which Paul and his party had brought from the Gentile congregations. Luke's omission of all mention of this ceremony, the chief reason for Paul's undertaking the perilous journey to Jerusalem, may indicate that Paul, who had set such great store by this visible demonstration of Gentile generosity and grace, found himself bitterly disappointed. On the other hand, the rapid movement of the narrative may disguise a time-lapse, and James may be absolved from the reproach of turning too hastily to the question of suspicions held concerning Paul, and from any suggestion of undue compulsion applied to the apostle.

The Jerusalem leaders were, of course, in a difficult position. They had been a small and menaced group when they had gone so far to conciliate the Gentile section of the Church. Over the ten years which lay between much had changed. Such men as Peter and Barnabas were finding increasing pre-occupation abroad on their unrecorded missionary journeys. Their broad and steadying influence was no longer felt in Jerusalem. The active work of Judaizing missionaries shows that, almost from the beginning, the Jerusalem decree lacked unanimous acceptance and the years had seen the consolida-tion of the opposition. The Gentile church had grown large and powerful, and jealousy, that fundamental Jewish, indeed human, fault, was a factor in policy. The Jerusalem church had also grown in numbers, but its accretions had been predomi-nantly from Pharisaic elements, and those who saw no need to abandon Judaism because of their acceptance of what they believed to be Judaism's fulfilment in Christ. Hence the touch of anxiety in James' appeal to Paul. The Gentiles, he hints (25), had won a great concession. Let Paul, therefore, set Jewish minds at rest by publicly demonstrating that his Gentile ministry had not destroyed his Jewish loyalties, and that he was happy to promote the efforts of Jewish Christians to maintain the practices of their ancient faith.[1]

In examining the wisdom of Paul's compromise, it is important to remember that the writer of 1 Corinthians xiii was always anxious to correct what he felt to be an over-vehement strain in his own nature, and willing ever to make every legitimate adjustment 'to gain them that are under the law'. Indeed that whole utterance (1 Cor. ix. 19-23) absolves Paul from too closely pressed a charge of inconsistency. He had

---

[1] See C. H. Dodd, *Moffatt Commentary on Romans*, p. 233: 'He persuaded Paul—or rather, ordered him—to make a demonstration of his faithfulness.'

not yet realized what an irreconcilable menace Judaism was to be to the Church. He saw a battle ahead, as he told the Ephesian elders, but he was fresh from a triumph in Corinth. Nor could he know that the supremacy of the Jerusalem church which he, going a magnanimous second mile, had sanctioned, was to be swept away along with the rebellious, stiff-necked city herself in the gale of the next decade's history. It seemed prudent to meet James' request, and Paul must have been deeply weary of the conflict with his one-time fellow-Pharisees who, after all, had come some distance to meet him. He sought to love, to understand, to act in selfless humility. The result, by that tragic irony which Heaven sometimes permits, was apparent disaster.

b. The riot (xxi. 27-39)

This fine piece of terse writing can only be the work of an eye-witness. With their eyes on the Christian Pharisees, whose Judaistic sensitivities they sought over-tenderly to soothe, James and Paul himself appear to have overlooked the old foes, *the Jews which were of Asia* (27). Ephesus had already demonstrated the potentialities of mob-violence, and the Jews of that city shared with their Hellenic neighbours a proneness to riot and civil tumult. Crying havoc against Paul, they succeeded in stirring such a disturbance that the garrison, stationed in the Tower of Antonia overlooking the area, was forced to intervene. A strong detachment descended one of the two stairways and drove violently through the crowd to the rescue, under the impression that an Egyptian-Jewish charlatan, who had already caused a most serious outbreak, had appeared again.

A tribune was a considerable officer, and Claudius Lysias appears to have been one of the career men of the days of Pallas and Narcissus. He was a Greek as his second name shows. His first name must have been assumed when he was granted Roman citizenship, 'at a great price' (xxii. 28) under the rule of the venal Greek freedmen of the Emperor Claudius. Paul may have been fortunate in the officer he encountered.

None the less, Lysias was a vigorous and capable soldier, and the rescue was effected with precision and success.

It is possible to gain some impression of the person and presence of the prisoner. Paul did not reveal his Roman citizenship until the conclusion of his speech. It is obvious that he must have possessed a commanding personality for a senior officer to pause in the midst of a perilous situation, and to allow a prisoner, whom he had just snatched from the hands of a passionately excited mob, to stand on the stairs leading to safety, and address the multitude over the fence of the soldiers' spears. It is interesting to see Paul reveal his heirship to the triple tradition of European culture. His Greek first caught the tribune's attention. He addressed the crowd in their Hebrew dialect. He was soon to claim his Roman privileges.

c. Paul's speech (xxi. 40–xxii. 24)

Nothing more clearly indicates Paul's fine education and superb powers of mind than his ability to make immediate and effective contact with any audience, and to present his message, without loss of content, in the terms of their thought and experience. It was a remarkable feat of intellectual balance and self-control after the violence of the mob's man-handling, and a rescue which can have taken little thought of gentleness, to lay hold of the opportunity for testimony, and in the act assess the needs of the situation and the appropriate approach. Paul casts aside all theology and bases his defence on the facts of personal experience. In spite of the stinging injustice he had suffered, and the ungodly violence of the crowd's attack from which he was still reeling, he does all he possibly can do to conciliate his hostile audience. *I was zealous toward God*, he says, *as ye all are this day* (3). Ananias, he remarks, was *a devout man according to the law, having a good report of all the Jews* (12). He postpones as far as possible a reference to the Gentiles by name (21). In verse 15 he even modifies the Lord's words (ix. 15) to this end. He was bound, however, to speak the whole truth, and there came a place in his address, as there did at Athens, when no art of oratory or grace of language could cover up the point and thrust of the speaker's challenge. Tumult blazed forth again, which Luke appears to have viewed from some vantage-point. Perhaps he was on the steps with Paul. He saw the wildly-tossing garments and the flung dust. At a sharp word the soldiers closed in, and the detachment climbed the stairs. 'Thus was St. Paul at last', writes R. B. Rackham,[1] 'delivered into the hands of the Gentiles, and into bondage which will last five years.'

d. In the hands of Rome (xxii. 25-29)

This interesting paragraph shows the authority of imperial Rome in action. Probably with little or no understanding of his Aramaic, the tribune had allowed Paul to speak, and may have been both alarmed and annoyed when the speech suddenly provoked a wild outburst from the crowd. Hustled into safety in the guard-room, Paul was handed over to a responsible centurion, one of that sturdy officer class who move so worthily through the pages of the New Testament that one is prompted to believe that the difficult garrison-duty in Palestine was regarded as an assignment for picked men. As the soldiers bound his limbs for the frightful experience of scourging Paul mentioned his Roman citizenship. The claim was immediately taken seriously, for it was as serious an offence to disregard it as to make it without factual foundation. Hence the perturbation at Philippi, and the more dignified concern shown in the well-conducted headquarters of Jerusalem. The commander called for a solemn affidavit (27), and, when this was given, relaxed sufficiently before his prisoner to contrast a little wistfully his own hard-won citizenship with that to which Paul had been born in Tarsus.[2] The punishment squad was summarily dismissed, and Lysias showed that solicitude which was natural in a man who had won status and office by obvious ability and drive, but against a precarious background of events which could never have been far from his thoughts.

[1] *Op. cit.*, p. 420.
[2] Ramsay, *The Cities of St. Paul*, pp. 169 ff.

e. Before the Sanhedrin (xxii. 30–xxiii. 9)

'For the fifth time, the Sanhedrin, the supreme court of the Jews, had to adjudicate upon the claims of the new Kingdom of God.'[1] Anxious to fulfil all the requirements of justice, and in pursuance of that careful policy towards the Jews which Pilate's clumsy handling of the race had more than ever commended to his successors, the commander had judged it wise to set Paul before the tribunal of his own people. The proceedings in the disciplined Roman guard-house must have appeared to Paul strikingly more proper than the irregular conduct of the Jewish religious assembly. Hence the vehemence of his reaction against the high priest (3). How it came about that he failed to identify the petty tyrant is a matter of some conjecture. He had, of course, been absent for some time from Jerusalem, and might not necessarily assume that the chairman of the assembly was the supreme religious functionary. If his sharp retort contrasted with his Lord's forbearance under similar provocation, it conformed to conduct which most readers of the very human story will readily recognize.

Summing up the situation, and despairing of justice, Paul saw that this was not a time or place for constructive argument and defence. He boldly claimed the protection of his class, and won it. It is sometimes thought that Paul's action in dividing his audience was a clever stroke of policy, and a not very creditable attempt to avoid the main issue and gain a stump-orator's victory. F. W. Farrar[2] takes this view. 'We cannot defend his conduct', he writes. 'He was a little unhinged, both morally and spiritually, by the wild and awful trials of the day before.' The claim still to be a Pharisee 'was hardly worthy of Saint Paul. . . .' In his brilliant essay on the statesmanship of Paul, Ramsay[3] answers this criticism conclusively. It is true that the event on the Damascus road shattered and rebuilt Paul's life. Never was conversion so complete and so transforming. But it is also correct to say, as Ramsay maintains,

---

[1] R. B. Rackham, *op. cit.*, p. 427.
[2] *The Life and Work of St. Paul*, p. 541.
[3] *Pauline Studies*, pp. 83–100.

that, when Paul came to look over the whole course of his life, and to reflect calmly on the plan which was so clearly woven into it, he saw that continuity and unfolding purpose to which he often makes reference. He had been separated, he claims, 'from his mother's womb' (Gal. i. 15) for the task before him. *Brethren*, he said, in the moment before the high priest's interruption, *I have lived in all good conscience before God until this day* (1). So again in his defence before Felix, he was to claim that, as a Christian, he was 'serving the God of our fathers, believing all things that are according to law ... always exercising myself to have a conscience void of offence towards God and men' (xxiv. 14–16). These statements do not conflict with those in which he speaks of revolution in his life. 'His defence was always the same', says Ramsay, 'and therefore carefully planned: that his life had been consistently directed towards one end, the glorification of the God of Israel by admitting the Nations to be His servants, and that this was true Judaism and true Pharisaism.' Hence the relevance of the defence before the Sanhedrin. 'If one party', Ramsay continues, 'was more capable of being brought to a favourable view of his claims than the other he would naturally and justifiably aim at affecting the minds of the more hopeful party.' That is exactly what Paul did at Athens, when he addressed himself almost exclusively to the Stoic element in his audience. He was claiming, moreover, 'to represent the true line of development in which Judaism ought to advance'. The Jewish faith, he was arguing, was sinking below its true self because it was atrophied and resisting the forces which impelled it forward. Paul's occasional compromises with Judaism have been noted above (xvi. 3, xviii. 18, xxi. 26). Perhaps they, too, should be viewed in the light of this philosophy, and set within the context of a growing conviction in Paul's mind that his life, after all, was a unity. Paul at first sight would be labelled as a Sadducee. He had belonged of old to that active Pharisaic wing which co-operated with the Sadducees in the suppression of Christianity. To the multitude at large, seeking a classification for his cosmopolitan attitude, his alleged contempt for the Law, and his rejection of Jewish isolationism, it would appear at once that his allegiance lay with the sacerdotal party. What more obvious exordium therefore than to claim his Pharisaic status, developed and purified, and to reject all identification with the party erroneously associated with him by proclaiming faith in a doctrine they rejected, and a doctrine, furthermore, peculiarly Christian.[1]

f. Rome intervenes (xxiii. 10–35)

Paul had passed through two days of fearful mental, spiritual, and physical stress. Twice the intervention of a Roman military patrol had rescued him from the violence of his own compatriots. He was no doubt assailed with misgivings, and the recollection of the warnings which had punctuated his journey to Jerusalem would arise to torment him. Abraham had once known a like experience. Without measuring consequences he had flung his shepherd guerrillas on an invading force from the Euphrates and knew full well that he had routed them by surprise. Under the spur of the saintly Melchizedek's approval he had rejected with scorn the goods Sodom offered. In the night came fear, and the collapse of confidence. . . . And God appearing said: 'Fear not, Abram: I am thy shield, and thy exceeding great reward' (Gn. xv. 1). The Abraham of the New Testament, a prey to similar doubts, is in the same fashion encouraged (11).

The hate of Paul's enemies reached its climax in the vow to kill him (12). There is no need to picture these scoundrels starving to death when frustrated of their purpose. The scribes and lawyers were experts in sophistic devices of escape, and there was certainly some formula of absolution by which the hungry and thirsty conspirators would be able in due course to escape from the worst consequences of their oath. The plot throws a flash of light on Paul's family. If the secret plotting of the Jewish leaders was known to Paul's sister, the family must have had the highest connections. The brave lad who was Paul's nephew is also pleasant to meet.

[1] Ramsay, *Pauline Studies*, pp. 91–94.

The story of Lysias' security measures makes the section an important historical document. Palestine was recognized as a stormy province, and the need for a special policy and unusual adaptations in the government of the Jews was acknowledged by the Roman authorities. The narrative has already revealed the alertness of the garrison in dealing with an outbreak of mob-violence, accompanied by striking deference on the part of the senior officer towards the Sanhedrin. Nine or ten years later the country erupted in passionate revolt. It is evident that the Romans were aware of the simmering heat beneath the surface when 470 troopers of the Jerusalem garrison were detached at a moment's notice to escort one prisoner to the provincial headquarters.

Claudius Lysias' letter is interesting reading. The tribune takes a slight liberty with truth and advances the hour of his regard for Paul's Roman citizenship. It made a neater story, set the officer in a slightly more favourable light, and is altogether in character. Felix, the corrupt brother of Claudius' freedman Pallas, was married to Drusilla, daughter of Herod Agrippa 1. *Cilicia* (34) was included in Syria, and the legate of Syria was Felix' immediate superior. He was therefore competent to try the case as a deputy. Felix was procurator of Judaea from AD 52 to AD 56 or 58 but had held a military command in Palestine previous to this term of office. Hence 'many years' in xxiv. 10.

Additional Notes

xxi. 15. AV *carriages* means, of course, 'baggage', an Elizabethan use. It seems, however, demonstrable that the phrase can mean 'having equipped horses', that is having hired mounts and pack animals. Two days were available for a 64-mile journey to Jerusalem, and this rendering makes sense in the context of the narrative.

xxi. 20. *They are all zealous of the law.* A strong verb is used signifying a basic state or condition. 'They are all first and foremost zealots of the Law.' In other words, James implies that the Christianity of the Pharisaic wing was built upon an unmodified Judaism.

xxi. 31, 32. See the RV for a touch of literal vividness in the translation which neatly reflects the Greek.

xxi. 39. It has been noted that Paul's famous phrase *a citizen of no mean city* is an echo of a line of Euripides (*Ion*, 8) applied to Athens. The Tarsians were possibly in the habit of appropriating the quotation.

xxii. 13. Ananias 'came and stood over me, and said. . . .' Luke used the same verb in his story of Martha and Mary (Lk. x. 40) where AV shrinks from translating it. 'Martha came and *stood over* Jesus and Mary and said. . . .'

xxiii. 24. Tacitus' scornful chapter (*Ann.* xii. 54) on Felix makes interesting comment on the Roman into whose hands Paul was now delivered.

XV. CAESAREA (xxiv. 1–xxvi. 32)

a. The charges against Paul (xxiv. 1–9)

A few words only of Tertullus' elaborate oration are given, but enough to reveal the nature of his rhetoric and the character of his accusation. Luke has a remarkable aptitude for using thus a brief quotation. It is not unlikely that the orator was a Roman, for there is a Latin ring about some of his phrases as they appear in Luke's Greek, and his name, although this does not necessarily indicate nationality, is Latin. He was certainly trained in the arts of contemporary rhetoric, and what impressed Luke was his elaborate exordium, a *captatio benevolentiae*, or 'seeking of goodwill', as the theorists termed it. Such a subterfuge, says Calvin, is 'a sign of a bad conscience'. It was rather traditional courtesy, and the device, albeit purged of mendacity and sycophancy, is to be distinguished in the opening gambit of Paul's reply (10).

The charges made followed those levelled against Christ Himself, and fall similarly under three heads. First, Paul was *a pestilent fellow, and a mover of sedition among all the Jews throughout the world* (5). This amounted to a charge of treason, or *laesa maiestas*. This crime lacked precise definition in Roman law, and became a device under tyrannical emperors for political terrorism. Authoritarian régimes have at all times been noted for the employment of elastic legal safeguards of the sort. In days of good government the law of treason found no exercise, but it was always prone to revival. At the time of Christ's trial, and similarly of Paul's, it was a dangerous charge, and easily invoked against a person whose actions or words could be constructed as a menace to the tranquillity of the community. Under Felix, Tertullus had already stated that the land had enjoyed *great quietness* (2). For all the corruption of Felix' régime, attested by both Tacitus[1] and Josephus,[2] and the irritant his personality had proved in the affairs of Palestine, the governor had endeavoured to deal with banditry and other disturbances of the peace. It was subtle to suggest to him that the present proceedings formed an occasion for the furtherance of his good work, and provided a cheap opportunity, *in corpore uili*, to offset some of the other abuses of his régime. Secondly, Paul was set down as a ring-leader of the Nazarenes, a group without official recognition, and by implication dissident and rebellious. Finally, he had profaned the temple, the one charge on which the Jews appear to have been able even to put a Roman to death. Tertullus backed his accusations with the testimony of eyewitnesses (9).

b. Paul's reply (xxiv. 10–21)

Paul deals first with the charge which he regarded as most serious, that he was a disturber of Rome's peace (11–13). He had faced this ill-defined but perilous accusation in Philippi and Thessalonica, and he met it with plain facts. Nowhere had he stirred up the people, nor could the accusers prove that he had (12, 13). Paul answers insincerity and falsehood point by point with devastating clarity. It was in no mood of rebellion

[1] *Ann.* xii. 54; *Hist.* v. 9.
[2] *B.J.* xii, xiii, xiv.

and violence, he points out, that he had come to Jerusalem and the temple, but in a spirit of lowly worship. He had, in fact, brought monetary aid for the distressed of his people, and had visited the shrine for purposes related to their faith. He had initiated no debate nor provoked the crowd. As for the Asian Jews who figured in the incident, and whose false information was behind Tertullus' indictments (5), it was significant, surely, that they were not produced in court. It was true, said Paul, that he worshipped the God of his fathers after the fashion of *the way* (14), which was nothing more than the name implied, and involved no abandonment of the old revelation. It was no 'sect' (RV) for all their tendentious language.

It was also true, said Paul, continuing his damaging admissions, that he had annoyed Ananias, present in the court, by the bold affirmation of a doctrine abhorrent to that priest. Felix was left to determine the relevance of this. Paul's statement was not 'a confession of error', as F. W. Farrar[1] described it, or 'the honest admission of a mistake', as F. J. Foakes-Jackson[2] described it half a century later. It was a most effective closing point, and it is the commentator last quoted who remarks that Tarsus possessed a famous law school.[3] The whole defence illustrates the apostle's astonishing ability to speak according to the occasion, and Luke's ability as a reporter.

c. Felix (xxiv. 22-27)

Convinced by Paul's defence, but like Pilate wary of the Jews and willing to 'show them pleasure' (27), Felix deferred the case, a stratagem which suited him, and was the utmost satisfaction the disconcerted prosecution could hope to gain. Felix also had an eye to possible gain, and there has been some speculation about the considerable funds which must have been at Paul's disposal over this period of his life.[4] Perhaps, too, Paul had stirred some movement in that corrupt mind.

---

[1] *The Life and Work of St. Paul*, p. 543.
[2] *Op. cit.*, p. 217.
[3] *Ibid.*
[4] Ramsay, *St. Paul the Traveller and Roman Citizen*, pp. 310-312.

Drusilla, Felix' girl-wife, must have discussed the matter with him. She may have had knowledge of her father's unfortunate relations with earlier Christians, and desired to hear their greatest, or most notorious preacher. 'Righteousness, self-control, and judgment to come' (25) were, however, the last themes calculated to soothe either the governor or his wife. Righteousness had small part in Felix' administration; self-control was not prominent in the court-favourite who had persuaded the young Jewess at his side to abandon her husband, Azizus, King of Emesa. And judgment to come was too direct a reminder, even to a man who took little thought of the hereafter, of that summons to Rome and a last accounting, which ultimately befell him. Felix was tangled in a web of evil circumstance of his own weaving, and the time was not convenient to cut himself boldly free (25).

d. Festus (xxv. 1–12)

With the coming of Felix' successor the implacable hatred of the Sadducees renewed its attempt to break through the Roman shield. The governor dismissed the application a little peremptorily. The trial should be held, he said, in Caesarea. 'Let them therefore . . . which are of power among you (RV; not *which among you are able*, as AV), go down with me, . . . let them accuse him' (5). The weary trial was therefore repeated, with the same three charges which Paul had already answered. Festus' business-like management is nevertheless apparent. His proposal to Paul (9) was equivalent to acquitting the prisoner on any charge which could come under his jurisdiction. Festus was, it may be assumed, under orders to handle his difficult provincials with care, and it was reasonable enough to suggest that the religious charges might still appropriately be heard before the proper authorities, with the governor himself present to ensure no miscarriage of justice. In other words, would Paul accept an acquittal on one count, and submit to a formal investigation before his people in matters they seemed to regard as important?

At this point Paul reached a crisis. He decided to exercise

his full rights as a Roman citizen. He refused to recognize the validity of the Jewish charges against him, or the competence of the sacerdotal court. The Roman authorities had held him in custody for two years. It was high time they pressed a charge against him or released him. If Festus was understood to say that no such charge was laid, but found himself inhibited by Roman-Jewish policy from just and decisive action, Paul proposed to release the governor from all embarrassment, and himself from the danger of assassination, by resort to the final court of appeal open to every Roman, that of Caesar himself.

Appellatio, to which process Paul thus resorted, was the act by which a litigant disputes a judgment, and the effect was that the case was brought before a higher magistrate, normally the one who had originally appointed the magistrate of the lower court. The litigant either pronounced the word *appello*, as Paul did here (11), or submitted his appeal in writing to the court of the magistrate whose judgment was impugned. That magistrate in either case was under obligation to transmit the file together with a personal report (*litterae dimissoriae*) to the competent higher magistrate. Hence, probably, there was some measure of embarrassment for Festus when, after consultation with his board of assessors (12), he accepted the appeal. He had virtually acquitted the prisoner, and, as a newcomer, had no exact knowledge of the religious situation out of which the charge had arisen. He must have been at a loss how to phrase the letter which was to accompany the appellant to the imperial court, and the terms of the communication to a tribunal so exalted as Caesar's were a matter of some importance, if only to the reputation of the magistrate concerned.

e. Agrippa II (xxv. 13-27)

At this point Herod Agrippa II, brother of Bernice and Drusilla, and great-grandson of the sinister tyrant of the Gospels, paid an official visit of welcome to the new governor. Festus seized the chance to secure an independent Jewish opinion on the case, especially since he had found that the

doctrine for which Paul was called in question had divided
Jewish opinion, and that, furthermore, a specific person was
associated with it (19), whose name had once divided Jewish
opinion yet more catastrophically. Agrippa himself professed a
keen desire to hear Paul, and the event became something of a
state occasion, with the puppet-king proceeding to the place of
audience *with great pomp* (23). It was in Caesarea that his
father, Agrippa I, had sat upon his throne arrayed in royal
apparel to receive the Tyrian deputation and listen to the
outrageous flatteries of the crowd (xii. 21). The taste for show-
manship had obviously descended to the son. Luke is again
correct in the title. Agrippa was the last Jewish king in Palestine. Bernice, his queen, was a worthy sister of Drusilla.[1]

Paul was not insincere in welcoming the opportunity to put
his case before the philo-Roman king. For three generations a
tradition of close liaison had linked the Herodian house with
the rulers of Rome, and with Festus' report pending, it was a
matter of some importance to secure from Agrippa any goodwill which clear and honest truthfulness could win. Besides,
as R. B. Rackham[2] remarks, of all the Herod line, 'Agrippa II
comes out the best. The Lord would not open His lips before
Antipas; nor would Paul give an exposition of his faith before
Drusilla. But before Agrippa II the apostle makes his most
elaborate apologia pro vita sua; he bears witness to the king's
Jewish faith; he had even hope of winning him to Christianity.
It is true that Agrippa somewhat cynically warded off Paul's
advances, but had he been as morally worthless as the other
Herods, we feel sure that the apostle would have adopted a
different tone.'

f. Paul's testimony (xxvi. 1-23)

It is tempting to believe that Luke was present in some
capacity at this interview. The account seems to bear the marks
of a first-hand report with scene and word stamped quite
indelibly on the writer's mind. Luke has caught Paul's

[1] Tacitus, *Hist.* ii. 81; Suetonius, *Tit.* vii; Josephus, *B.J.* ii.
[2] *Op. cit.*, p. 458.

characteristic gesture (1), the tone of the rather pompous king, courteously allowed by the Roman governor to take precedence in the hearing, and Paul's own exquisitely appropriate opening paragraph (2, 3)—his *captatio benevolentiae*. A strong, compelling memory, and the desire to do justice to a great occasion, could also be the reason for the reporting, for the third time in the book, of Paul's conversion. In this connection the essential harmony of the three accounts should be stressed. The slight variations are of no consequence.

Luke's preoccupation is to show that, in complete agreement with Festus whose virtual acquittal three times enters the narrative, the Jewish king found no fault in the prisoner. It was important for him to show that expert and independent Jewish opinion, equally with the verdict of Roman law, acquitted Paul of all misdemeanour. And the chapter would have been strangely out of balance without a full outline of the defence. Paul's testimony adds a few details appropriate to the occasion. It especially stresses the systematic nature of the attempt of the Sanhedrin to eradicate the Christians, and the dogged and devoted support the cruel campaign had received from the unconverted apostle. The matter was stressed because it emphasized the reality of the vision on the Damascus road, and that vision was vital to the doctrine of resurrection which Paul had felt constrained to stress since his interview with the Sanhedrin.

g. The verdict (xxvi. 24–32)

Paul was heard without impatience while he confined his argument to the abstract consideration of theological dogma. It was when he spoke specifically of an historic Christ, raised from the dead within living memory, that the audience grew restless. Something like the same situation had developed in Athens. Festus, thoroughly irritated, broke in with a rudeness at variance with the correct bearing which had so far done him credit. (His remark surely had a brusqueness about it which disallows Ramsay's[1] milder interpretation: 'Paul, Paul,

---

[1] *St. Paul the Traveller and Roman Citizen*, p. 313.

you are a great philosopher but you have no common sense.')
Perhaps gently to remind the Roman that he had surrendered
the occasion to his royal guest, Paul answered him with
courtesy, but directed his appeal specifically to Agrippa, only
to embarrass that person by claiming that he was far from
ignorant of the matters under discussion, and by an urgency
which provoked the king to terminate proceedings. It would
appear that Greek had been the language of the hearing, and
if it could be assumed that Agrippa's Greek was not of the
best, the difficulty occasioned by his remark (28) would at
least be explained. The AV certainly mistranslates it. The RSV
may translate its chosen reading correctly: 'In a short time
you think to make me a Christian!' If we translate, somewhat
doubtfully, 'In short, you think to make me a Christian', we
have at least words consonant with the occasion, and expressing
the royal impatience at Paul's clear intention. Paul's reply
would then be a play on words: 'In short or at length, no
matter, but I could wish one and all present stood where I
stand—save, of course,' he added ruefully, 'for these bonds.'

It may finally be asked whether Luke was justified in de-
voting so much of his limited space to Paul's examinations
before the various tribunals of Rome. Paul's case, it should be
remembered, was a test case. If he was finally acquitted, and
the Pastoral Epistles are solid evidence that he was, Luke's
final purpose is clear. Rome, however Nero later disregarded
the decision of the imperial court, had granted by the process
of this trial a charter of liberty to Christian evangelism. 'This
charter was indeed', writes Ramsay,[1] 'overturned by later
decision of the supreme court, but its existence was a highly
important fact for the Christians. . . .'

Early in the sixties of the first century it was possible for men
of insight to observe the setting of the stage for the clash
between Rome and the Church. It was important to have at
hand 'a temperate and solemn record, by one who had played
a great part in them, of the real facts regarding the formation

[1] *Ibid.*, pp. 308, 309.

of the Church, its steady and unswerving loyalty in the past, its firm resolve to accept the facts of imperial government, its friendly reception by many Romans, and its triumphant vindication in the first great trial at Rome. It was the work of one who had been trained by Paul to look forward to Christianity becoming the religion of the empire and the world, who regarded Christianity as destined not to destroy but to save the empire.'

Additional Notes

xxiv. 12. 'Stirring up a crowd' (RV) is not a correct translation of the most acceptable reading (*episustasis*). The noun means 'making a crowd collect', an easy proceeding in the Middle East. Paul's cogent point is that he had so conducted himself that a crowd had not found in unusual or provocative word or action on his part a focal point of gathering.

xxiv. 14. The AV *after the way which they call heresy* too boldly reads into the Greek word the later meaning which it acquired, and which dominates its derivative. The word *hairesis* is connected with the verb *haireō* which, in the middle voice, means 'to choose'. *Hairesis*, therefore, means a 'sect' (RV), a classification, that is, which one chooses by conviction or belief. The AV translates the word as 'sect' in xxvi. 5, where it contains no notion of dissidence. It is possible that the present context contains the germ of the pejorative meaning which the word later acquired by its prevailing use on the part of a majority to describe a minority, a situation, in human affairs, always likely to produce contempt or disapproval.

xxiv. 16. *I exercise myself*, says Paul, and uses a word (*askeō*) which occurs nowhere else in the New Testament. The word 'ascetic' is derived from it, but Paul implies no meaning of ordered or unnatural rigour. He refers to the discipline of life proper to Christian morality, and the watchfulness which is its salutary accompaniment. The word basically means 'to practise' or 'to train'. Paul sees himself as God's athlete.

xxiv. 22. The verse might be rendered: 'And when Felix,

who had a fairly accurate knowledge of Christian things, heard this, he adjourned the court, saying, I will go thoroughly into your case when the tribune Lysias comes down.'

xxv. 21. Augustus was the honorary title bestowed on Octavian, the first Emperor, in 27 BC. It was a Latin adjective of some religious significance, not previously used as a proper name. Like Caesar, it became a dynastic term and was held by every succeeding Emperor except Vitellius.

xxv. 23. *Pomp* in Greek is *phantasia*, and F. F. Bruce (*op. cit.*, p. 437) points to the linguistic curiosity that 'fantasia' is still used in Palestinian Arabic for a procession.

xxv. 26. . . . *unto my lord.* This title took sinister colouring in later use. In Egypt and the East, the Ptolemies, whose dynasty inherited the divine honours paid of old to the Pharaohs, were called 'Kurios' or 'lord'. From Nero onwards it appears more frequently in inscriptions. An Armenian puppet honoured Nero as 'master and god', and there is no doubt that, by the middle of the first century, that habit of ascription of divine honour to the Roman ruler was world-wide, and established.

xxvi. 4. Quoting Blass on this verse, F. F. Bruce (*ibid.*, p. 441) notes a preoccupation with Attic forms in Paul's speech. He neglected no art to commend his message, and would have seen no virtue in careless, or unpolished speech. To be 'all things to all men' presupposes an endeavour to speak the language of the audience, and to develop thought and argument within the framework of the hearers' experience. Deliberately to neglect this duty smacks of arrogance.

xxvi. 11. *To blaspheme* no doubt means to pronounce a formal curse on Christ. This was the dastardly ritual of the persecutor. Pliny (*Ep.* x. 96) remarks, in describing his repression of the Church in Bithynia some sixty years later, that no true Christian can be compelled *maledicere Christo*.

xxvi. 25. The word *soberness* answers Festus' petulant accusation of insanity. The Greek word has no reliable English equivalent. It is *sōphrosune*. To translate it, as the New Testament does, by 'soberness', 'moderation', 'self-control', 'temperance' is to touch its meaning from various angles, but not to cover it. The word has two roots, an adjective root meaning 'safe' and a noun root meaning 'mind'. It meant in Greek that ideal balance of thought which never flew to extremes. It is implicit in Paul's survey of Christian virtue in Romans xii where it may be rendered 'Christian sanity'. Notice, for example, verse 3: 'For as God in his grace has enabled me, I charge every one of you not to think more of himself than he ought to think, but to cultivate Christian sanity, according as God has given to every man faith as a measure.'

XVI. ON TO ROME (xxvii. 1–xxviii. 31)

a. The voyage and the storm (xxvii. 1–26)

A group of prisoners had collected at the headquarters at Caesarea, and Paul was sent on his journey to Rome along with them in charge of a centurion detailed for the task. The *frumentarii*,[1] or special military agents of the Emperor, sent abroad on duties of inspection, seem to have been a later invention; but information is far from complete, and those[2] who regard the otherwise unidentified *Augustus' band* (1) as a corps of picked troops detached from the regular formations for special services, may indeed be correct. It is not likely that the writer of the superbly told story which follows would err in a detail of nomenclature, so the *Augustus' band* must find its place in the list of known legionary formations.[3] The centurion, who was such a credit to the corps, was a capable officer whose simple decency and manliness (3, 43) recall other members of his class appearing in the New Testament (xxii. 26, xxiv. 23).

Paul's companions were Luke, and the obscure but faithful

[1] H. Mattingly, *Roman Imperial Civilisation*, pp. 123, 132.
[2] R. J. Knowling, *op. cit.*, ii, p. 516.
[3] Ramsay, *St. Paul the Traveller and Roman Citizen*, p. 315.

Aristarchus (xix. 29, xx. 4; Col. iv. 10; Phm. 24). The *ship of Adramyttium* (2), the seaport on the Aegean opposite Lesbos, was the likeliest vessel to put the party into the stream of trade from Asia to the west. They beat north along the difficult Palestinian coast to Sidon (2), and then, as the seasonal winds demanded, continued between Cyprus and the mainland (4) to Myra[1] in Lycia (5). Here the party transferred to an Alexandrian corn-ship which had perhaps chosen this northern route because of the lateness of the season (6). (Ramsay[2] is of the opinion that this was the regular route from Egypt.)

From Myra, at the extreme southern point of Asia Minor, the ship now proceeded west, making for Cnidus, a port at the south-west extremity of Asia Minor. They were unable to make the harbour for a wind off-land drove them south, and the shipmaster took refuge from it under the lee of the 140-mile long island of Crete (7). Fair Havens, where the ship found harbour, was (and is) a little more than half-way along this coast, just east of the part where the island rises into a group of lofty mountains. It was the old enemy, the north-east wind, funnelled down from these highlands (14) which drove them south from the more commodious harbour of Phenice, over twenty-three miles of turbulent sea, to the off-shore island of Clauda. Luke remembered vividly the struggle in which the passengers had aided the crew (16), when the brief advantage of the island's protection was seized to haul aboard the ship's boat, which was towing water-logged behind.

The storm was now heavy upon the lumbering vessel, as it came roaring out of the north-east. Far to the south, off the African coast, lay the notorious Syrtes (17), the graveyard of many ships, as underwater archaeology has vividly revealed in recent years. Hence the battle to maintain a westerly course, aided, it appears, by a veering of the wind to the east, as the cyclonic disturbance shifted its centre.

Paul's natural gifts of leadership are apparent. His responsible advice at Fair Havens was based on no little experience

[1] Freya Stark, *The Lycian Shore*, pp. 148-156.
[2] *St. Paul the Traveller and Roman Citizen*, p. 319.

(2 Cor. xi. 25), but had been thwarted by the shipowner's desire to land his wheat at Rome in good condition, and without adding a winter's sustenance to his overhead charges. Ramsay[1] is of the opinion that the ship was a government vessel of which the centurion, as senior officer, was properly in charge. This may have been the case, and if so the calculations upon which the shipmaster (not *owner* as AV and RV, according to Ramsay) based his rash advice are less apparent. Paul's leadership emerges again, at this climax of the storm, infused by his faith.

They were, indeed, at the end of human resource. They had looped and tautened cables precariously round the hull (17), to bind the straining timbers against the stress of the violent seas, and the leverage of the mast; they had cut loose all dispensable tackling and gear to lighten the vessel. It was a situation which must have reminded Paul of the psalmist's fears (cvii. 23–27). And it was all under a murky heaven (20) with the spray and driving cloud blotting out the stars, and the galley lumbering west at 35 to 40 miles a day. The whole company needed the divine comfort which came through Paul (21–26).

b. Shipwreck (xxvii. 27–44)

The end was coming rapidly. Hearing the sound of distant surf, the sailors suspected land or shoals ahead. The lead showed a shelving bottom, so the heavy bulk was hove to for the night with anchors out of the stern. This scheme kept the ship heading in the right direction before the pressure of the still driving wind. It was on the fairly transparent pretext of similarly anchoring the bow, that the crew proposed to launch the boat and escape to the shore, a plot frustrated by the alert apostle and a few quick sword-cuts on the ropes at the centurion's prompt orders.

Paul was clearly in moral control of the situation, and mingled an effective testimony with his practical suggestion about food. At this point a responsible officer seems to have

[1] *Ibid.*, pp. 323, 324.

numbered the ship's complement, a sensible measure in view of the necessity of getting everyone safely ashore (37). The rest of the night was spent in heaving overboard sacks of Egyptian wheat which formed the bulk of the cargo. With dawn appeared an unknown coast, a bay, and what appeared to be a practicable beach. A bar due to a cross-current frustrated the attempt to beach the vessel, which probably drew some eighteen feet of water, and it was at this point that the escort, who were responsible for the lives of the prisoners, proposed to kill them. The centurion's admiration for Paul is apparent in the refusal. After a struggle in the breakers over the inshore channel, the whole ship's company reached the safety of the beach. It was a triumph for Paul's faith and no small tribute to his dynamic personality.

c. Malta (xxviii. 1–10)

Malta, where the exhausted company now rested on the beach, was no abode of savages. The island had once been Carthaginian territory, and the peasantry still spoke the Phoenician language. The word *barbarian* (2, 4) in Greek simply meant one who spoke an unintelligible language, and contained no notion of uncouth or primitive culture. Verse 2 should be translated, 'The foreigners showed us no little kindness'. Paul, who had done so much to make the landing successful, was no laggard in the humbler task of gathering sticks, and in the course of this activity was fastened upon by a viper. No such reptiles live on Malta today. Within the last century they have similarly disappeared from Arran. Ireland, traditionally, saw a similar emancipation from the pest. Paul suffered no harm and the prestige he thus won served the company well (9, 10).

Again using the locally correct term for the Roman magistrate, Luke mentions a neighbouring country estate belonging to him, and here temporary shelter was provided. The excavation of numerous Roman villas in Britain has shown what large and self-contained institutions such establishments could be.

The medical colouring of this section has been noted by commentators, and Ramsay[1] has seen Luke's signature in verse 9. 'Paul healed Publius', he writes, 'but Luke is not said to have healed the invalids who came afterwards. They received medical attention.' By the last phrase, presumably, he would render *etherapeuonto*, which is represented in the AV by the words *were healed*. From whom would the crowds receive treatment but from 'Luke the physician'? Unfortunately for this attractive theory the same verb, in the same voice, mood, and tense is used in the story of Peter at v. 16 where no such medical attention is implied.

d. From Malta to Rome (xxviii. 11–15)

Three months later another Alexandrian ship, named after the patron deities of sailormen (11), and which had wintered at Valetta, took the company aboard. They proceeded to Italy by way of Syracuse, Rhegium and Puteoli. Puteoli was a great harbour, a nodal point on the imperial system of communications, and it is not surprising to find Christianity established there (14). If the Nazareth Decree is rightly interpreted as reflecting tension between Jew and Christian over the first Christian witness in Rome, the faith must have reached the capital in the fifth decade of the first century. Puteoli, like Corinth, Ephesus, and Antioch, was a centre of radiation.

From Puteoli the land-route to Rome was taken. Part of this journey was by barge through the Pontine Marshes, an uncomfortable and mosquito-ridden stage, if Horace,[2] who travelled south that way in 40 or 38 BC, is to be believed. The terminus of the canal was at Forum Appii where Roman Christians met the apostle.

Paul appears at this time to have been in a mood of discouragement. A tendency to low spirits, says Ramsay,[3] 'is always one of the most trying concomitants of his chronic disorder.' But it needs no supposed bout of malaria, which

---

[1] *Luke the Physician*, pp. 16, 17.
[2] *Sat.* i. 5.
[3] *St. Paul the Traveller and Roman Citizen*, p. 347.

indeed, if that malady was Paul's 'thorn', could have been stirred to activity in the Pontine Marshes, to explain a mood of apprehension at this crisis of a great career. Paul had passed through strenuous years, and a grim testing lay ahead in an unfamiliar environment. The landscape was harsh and the mighty city, cruel and hard, lay ahead. It would have been a less sensitive spirit than Paul's which could have faced a trial without temptation to despair. Christ stood by Paul at a crisis in his imprisonment (xxiii. 11). The same Presence had given courage on the tossing ship (xxvii. 23). And now the Christians of Rome played the role of comforter: Paul *took courage*. From Forum Appii, a place 'full of sailors and rascally inn-keepers' according to Horace in the poem already referred to, Paul moved on through the village of Three Shops to Rome. He was reaching the capital in a fashion vastly different from that which he had anticipated (Rom. i. 10–12), but there is no breath of self-pity in the account. Paul had his courage back.

e. At Rome (xxviii. 16–31)

Paul was allowed a measure of freedom over the two years which Luke now briefly records. The delay was due to the necessity for accusers to appear from Palestine, and for the hearing to find a place on Caesar's calendar. It is not unlikely that the case lapsed for want of accusation. It is known that later such situations were covered by a statute of limitations, but whether Paul was thus protected cannot be said. It would suit his enemies very well if they could leave him confined and in-active. Their hostility had already removed their enemy from active evangelism for three years. Nor is it unlikely that Festus' documents were lost in the wreck, and the necessity to secure duplicates would also occasion delay.

Paul settled down to a further test of patience and delay. Without discouragement and within the context of his pos-sibilities, he set to work on a programme of evangelism. The Jews, as usual, had the first opportunity. When Claudius' decree of exile (xviii. 2) had been rescinded is not known, but there is a subdued note in the comments of the Roman Jews which suggests a care to walk circumspectly in controversial matters such as those which had led to their banishment, and the disruption of their community. Reception was mixed and the book ends with Paul turning to the Gentiles.

The book ends abruptly.[1] It is inconceivable that the writer who had described with such art the speech before Agrippa would have abandoned the opportunity to describe the scene in Caesar's court, if indeed such a trial took place, and he had the facts or the living memory at his pen's disposal. Luke's work may have been tragically interrupted. Another book may have been projected beginning with release or acquittal in Rome, and proceeding with the story of further evangelism.

It was never written. After all, is the unfinished state of the book inappropriate? The work continues, and if the Acts of the Apostles ends by the Tiber, the acts of God through the dedicated lives of men found, and still find, a stage far wider in place and time.

Additional Notes

Comparison with other storm narratives in ancient literature will reveal the high standard of Luke's account in chapter xxvii of the wreck of the corn-ship. The curious might look up the following passages: Homer, *Od.* xii. 400–453; Vergil, *Aen.* i. 81–179; Juvenal, *Sat.* xii. 17–82; Josephus, *Vita* iii; Lucian, *Ship.* vii.

xxvii. 3. Literally, 'to the friends'. The phrase may contain one of the names by which the early Christians referred to members of their communities, based, if such is the case, on Jn. xv. 15 (cf. 3 Jn. 14).

xxvii. 9. There was a particularly dangerous period for autumn navigation, extending, according to Vegetius, the writer on military affairs (*De Re Mil.*, iv. 39), from mid-September to mid-November. After the latter date navigation ceased for the winter. F. F. Bruce, who dates this voyage in AD

---

[1] For contrary views see F. F. Bruce, *op. cit.*, p. 481 and F. J. Foakes-Jackson, *op. cit.*, p. 236.

59 (*op. cit.*, p. 455) calculates that 'the Fast' fell on October 5. But whatever the year, the Jewish dating suggests that the event lay in the middle of 'the dangerous period'.

xxvii. 17. The *helps* are frequently mentioned in ancient literature. 'See you not', writes Horace describing the labouring ship of state (*Od.* i. 14), 'that the side is stripped of oars, the masts crippled by the rushing south-west wind, the yard-arms groaning, and that without ropes the hull can scarcely weather the too peremptory sea?' Some references (e.g. Plato, *Rep.* x. 616C) leave doubt as to the precise process. It is possible that the hull, as the term implies, was undergirded, but that an extension of the cables formed a network above deck which could be twisted to tautness.

xxvii. 19. The sail was 'struck' and the 'tackling' thrown overboard, and in both phrases (17 and 19) the word 'gear' (*skeuos*) is used. It is probable that this is the long spar on which the main sail depended and which might become unmanageable in a storm.

xxvii. 27. *Adria* was not the Adriatic of today. This sea lay between Italy, Malta, Crete, and Greece, and may be geographically identified by references in Strabo (ii. 5. 20) and Pausanias (v. 25. 3). It is 'the gulf between Italy and the Balkan peninsula', extending as far as the seas east of Sicily (*O.C.D.*, p. 8). Liddell and Scott do not notice the use.

xxvii. 37. Josephus speaks of a ship in which he sailed for Rome with no less than 600 people aboard (*Vita* iii).

xxvii. 41. Literally 'the stern began to break up under the violence of the waves'. With the forepeak stuck hard in the mud there was an oscillation which soon tore apart the heavily tried and strained timbers.

xxvii. 44. The Greek text admits the possibility that some came ashore on the backs of, or by the aid of others. *Broken pieces*, as the italics indicate, is a guess of the AV.

xxviii. 3. Translate: 'And the natives of the island showed us quite unusual kindness. They lit a bonfire and brought us all to it, because of the rain which had set in and the cold.'

xxviii. 11. One of the functions of Castor and Pollux was the care of storm-bound ships. 'Soon as their white star has shone on sailormen', writes Horace (*Od.* i. 12. 27–32), 'the wind-driven spray streams down from the rocks, the winds fall and the clouds scud away, and on the sea the threatening wave, for that they have so willed it, sinks to rest.' In the thundery weather a pale blue electrical discharge sometimes plays round the masts of ships, called by Italian sailors 'St. Elmo's Fire'. This was thought to indicate the presence of the Dioscuri. As Macaulay wrote:

> *Safe comes the ship to harbour*
> *Through tempest and through gales,*
> *If once the great Twin Brethren*
> *Sit shining on the sails.*

What Paul thought of this is not recorded, but his shipwrecked companions may have cast eyes on the ship's 'sign' with a measure of superstitious comfort.

xxviii. 16. The *captain of the guard* was, in all likelihood, the powerful commander of the praetorians. Writing to Pliny as governor of Bithynia (*Ep.* x. 57) the Emperor Trajan directs: 'As to the person who was banished by Julius Bassus, but continued to remain in the province without making an appeal, for which he had two years' opportunity if he thought himself wrongly banished, I direct that he be sent in chains to the prefect of the Praetorians. . . .'

xxviii. 25. Cf. Mt. xiii. 12 ff.; Mk. iv. 12; Lk. viii. 10; Jn. xii. 39 f.; Rom. xi. 8. It was important to identify the action of the Jews as a fulfilment of prophecy.